The Organic
Grow it, Cook it, Preserve it Guidebook

The Organic
Grow it, Cook it,
Preserve it
Guidebook

By D X &
Barbara Fenten

GROSSET & DUNLAP
A National General Company
Publishers   New York

To Marty and Big Poppa—
Without whom, nothing

Preface

Need an excuse to try something different? Something you've always wanted to do? Write a book. We did and we're glad of it.

We had gardened before and, of course, we had eaten well before. But, we had never experienced the sense of satisfaction nor the unbelievable good eating that resulted from working on this book. We tried all sorts of new ways to grow things. Some were great successes—others dismal flops. We cooked and tested and tasted a variety of new (for us) recipes. Some we loved and put on our "regular" menu, others we hated and can do little more than ruefully remember. We gardened, we cooked, we preserved and we loved it.

So, our first acknowledgement and thank you goes to you our reader, for getting us to do what we should have done long ago. Next our thanks go to the gardeners, horticulturists, growers, manufacturers and suppliers who gave their expert help and advice every time we asked for it and sometimes when we didn't. Then to our friends and relatives who contributed favorite recipes, always with the advice, "Try it, you'll like it." Many, many other people became involved in this project and to all of them a heartfelt thank you.

All books are team efforts and this one is no exception. But this one is special because it is the first time that we will appear as coauthors. We hope it is a beginning.

Both of us wish to say a special and very public thanks to the other members of our families responsible for this book—to Donna and Jeff, who had to eat all the things we cooked and never knew what the next meal might bring, and to our parents who by the end of the summer were a little hesitant about accepting our invitation to come out for the weekend. But their help and enthusiasm really made it all possible. For that and for all the editing, typing and proofreading . . . our thanks.

D X and Barbara Fenten

Greenlawn, L. I. New York

Contents

Introduction

BEAUTIFUL. AROMATIC. MAGNIFICENT. Delicious. Succulent. These are just a few of the superlatives used to describe home-grown fruits and vegetables. But how can you describe the size, the color, the taste, the smell and the feel of produce that is both organically and home-grown? You can't! There are no words truly suitable for this description. Organically home-grown fruits and vegetables are "something else" and must be experienced to be appreciated.

And, that's only part of our story. Think of being able to serve the purest, most delightful-tasting fruits, berries, vegetables, salads, soups, entrees, jams, jellies and preserves. Learn to prepare them the way they taste best, not to mention the way they are best for you. All can be made and served simply and quickly using recipes and cooking suggestions that emphasize the fact that for these special fruits and vegetables, the best taste comes from the least cooking.

Anyone who has tried will agree: There is nothing in the world to equal the taste of fresh corn cooked and eaten minutes after picking. Or berries still warm from the sun. Or vegetables eaten raw while still covered with early morning dew. All this without insecticides, miticides, fungicides or other "cides" and chemicals. If this isn't Utopia, it's as close as we'll get for a long, long time.

There's a lot more to this story, too. This marvelous produce can be enjoyed all year long. In season and out of season. When it's hot and when it's cold. Almost all of the things grown in the garden can be preserved for later use. Some can be canned and some can be frozen. Some can be dried and some can be left as they are. Whichever way best suits you and your produce, the results will be the tastiest, most economical and "best for you" foods you have ever eaten.

A word of caution: Once you have grown, cooked and preserved your own fruits and vegetables you will never be able to enjoy any of these items bought in a supermarket or other store. There is no comparison. Many home gardeners never buy a store tomato, cucumber, green pepper or any other produce items once they have been spoiled by tasting the real thing.

And now some thoughts on the word "organic." To some it is a religion. To some it is a way of life. In this book the word is meant to mean a natural way of doing things, be it gardening, cooking or preserving. We are not interested in becoming what one lady called "organic food fanatics." We are interested in doing things the way they should be done—naturally. We do not suggest you use any chemical substances to help your garden grow or to ward off insects. We do not suggest you use any additives, chemicals or phony flavorings in your cooking. We do not suggest that you use any preservatives in your canning or preserving. Nor do we suggest you use raw sugar instead of granulated, wheat germ or crunchy granola instead of steak, or nuts and fruits instead of a well-balanced diet. We do suggest that you use common sense and the purest ingredients for everything you cook, serve and eat.

There is nothing especially new or startling in this book. Everything described here has been tried before, often thousands of times, and found to "work." When you try them you will make additions and deletions from our suggestions and recipes. That's fine, for all we want to do is get you started growing it, cooking it and preserving it.

CHAPTER 1

Gardening
the Natural Way

DIG A HOLE. Drop in a seed. Reap the harvest. Wouldn't it be
wonderful if it were true? Of course we all have heard the old
cliché: "What comes too easily is not valued very highly" . . . and
perhaps it is so. Besides the old cliché, there is also the fact that in
this jet age there are still some things you just can't hurry, and
working with the soil is one of them. After a while gardening
becomes almost therapeutic . . . almost magical. You work with
the earth, work with nature, and you have something to show for
it when you get through.

Before you get started, there are certain things you should
know about gardening. It can be a lot of fun, but it can also be a
lot of hard work. You should know that gardening takes time,
effort and some money. You should know that like most things
worth doing, it must be done well. And, you should also know
that organic gardening is well worth everything you put into it. It
repays you many times each year in beauty, satisfaction and
pleasure, and does all this without taking anything good away
from, or adding anything bad to, our Earth.

With this in mind, start thinking about your garden. What do
you want to grow? How big do you want your garden to be?
Where, on your property, will you put the garden? Who will do
most of the gardening? Many other questions will come to mind,
hopefully, as you start your next step—planning.

This is always a very difficult stage for us, sitting down and logically planning all the aspects of our garden. Once we get to thinking about our garden, we don't want to sit and plan. We want to get out and get started. But we have learned through years of gardening experience that the better we plan, the easier the work and the more efficient and productive the garden.

Start by answering all the questions you asked yourself while thinking about your garden. Size . . . only as large as you can care for without giving up an entire summer's Saturdays, Sundays and most other leisure time. If it is your first garden, don't make it so big you become a slave to it. A garden needs a lot of TLC (tender loving care) and there's only a limited amount around. Start small, and when the season is about over, say it should have been bigger. There is always next year. As tempting as everything in the seed catalogs may look . . . start small. Remember that with gardening, as with everything else, you learn by doing and you learn by making mistakes. It is far better to make small mistakes than big ones, and easier to learn in a small garden and apply the knowledge to a larger garden next year.

Location? If you live in a suburban area and have land, you will probably have no problem selecting a site for the garden. If you have a very small piece of property, start looking for places and ways in which you can get "two for the price (and space) of one." For example, use strawberries as a ground cover, and instead of having just an attractive ground cover, you'll have an attractive ground cover which bears luscious strawberries. Use blueberry bushes to form a hedge and you can add delicious berries to the other advantages provided by the hedge.

When trying to locate your garden on a large piece of property, use the process of elimination. First, keep your garden as close as possible to your back door. Eliminate those areas which are a bike ride away from your kitchen. Second, look for a spot that is in sunlight most of the day. Eliminate all areas shaded by the house, garage or trees. Third, find a spot that is level. Eliminate all areas where your vegetables would have to grow on a slant, slope or hill. Fourth, make certain your vegetables do not have to compete with hedges, large shrubs or trees. In almost every case where this competition exists, the vegetables come off second-best. Also eliminate all areas near to or surrounded by water and nutrient-seeking roots.

If there is any spot left after all this elimination, that's the place for your garden. About 500 square feet of this choice territory will do nicely as a starter garden for a family of four with "average" tastes in vegetables. If you can spare more than this 20- x 25-foot piece of land, good for you, but save it. Remember your promise about waiting for next year. Besides, some more of your property will be taken over by fruits and berries, so only start what you can finish without ending up exhausted.

What to plant? Start by planting only those vegetables that your family likes and eats. And, equally as important, plant only the amount you can use. Plan on giving some away to friends and relatives, preparing some for freezing and canning (a year-long treat) and, of course, the real reason for the whole thing, eating most of your produce as it comes from the garden.

There is another consideration as you jot down the vegetables you are going to grow in your garden—space. It may sound obvious, but it must be considered and it must be considered early in the game. For example, melons and other vine crops take up a lot more room than just about anything else. Corn, because you need at least five rows for pollination, requires a considerable amount of space. Unstaked tomatoes can also take up a lot of space.

The choice of vegetables may not be nearly as simple as it would seem. In addition to picking your favorites and picking according to the amount of space they require, add yet another important consideration—are they right for your area? Temperature, rainfall and length of growing season in your locality can often determine which plants shall prosper and which shall perish. Select only those vegetables and those varieties of vegetables that can grow and be harvested in your area without a lot of crossed fingers and praying for heavenly intervention. Seed catalogs and packets will give you this information.

Once all this thinking, planning and selecting are completed, you are finally ready to do something. The area you selected for your vegetable garden must first be made ready for planting. The best time to do this is in the fall, October or November, when the air is crisp and cool. Take a small shovelful of soil and check it. If a handful makes a firm ball or makes a gooey mudball, it's good for throwing, but not for planting or plowing. When the soil crumbles between your fingers it is ready to be worked.

If you have had a garden on this spot before, this turning under becomes a bit easier. If not, console yourself by repeating as you dig that this is the hardest you will ever have to work in your garden (unless of course you decide to enlarge it next year). Your children will probably envy this chance to play in the dirt so enjoy it and get the job done.

Whatever covers the area now—leaves, weeds, grass—must be turned under. The soil must be broken up and organic matter added. Turning under organic matter serves two purposes: as the organic matter breaks down and decomposes, it feeds the soil and changes its structure to one with a consistency (tilth) closer to the kind needed by plants if they are to grow and thrive. In short, you must get your soil into the best possible shape to accept your seeds and seedlings.

That, in a nutshell, is one of the main principles of organic gardening; if you want to take something out of the soil (vegetables, fruits and berries) you must be sure to put something into the soil (other organic matter). It stands to reason that if you continually take from the soil, and put nothing back, after a short time it will have nothing more to give and will become worthless for anything but walking on.

For plants to grow they must have oxygen and carbon dioxide (both in the air), hydrogen (from water along with additional oxygen), nitrogen, phosphorous, potassium and 13 other nutrients (all supplied by the soil). Those gardeners who want the easy way out add many of these nutrients to their soil by simply spreading any of dozens of commercially manufactured chemical fertilizers. But, that defeats one of the purposes of our growing our own food . . . how can you know what is in the food you are eating if you don't know what is in the fertilizer you are putting into the soil? All that is written on the bag is that it contains N, P, K, and other alphabet soup chemicals.

Organic gardeners feel you should always replace in kind whatever you take. If the vegetables, fruits and berries are organic, put organic matter back into the soil. That sounds easy enough, but what is organic matter and where do you get it? Everything that was once alive is considered to be organic and you get it wherever you can. Such things as leaves, weeds and grass clippings are easily available in suburban areas. They are full of nutrients and they are free. In addition, most garden stores or nurseries stock nitrogen-rich organic soil additives such as cottonseed meal, animal manures, blood meal and fish meal and emulsion. If you live near a farm or any place that owns animals you'll probably be able to get as much free manure as you can carry away. Some factories that process cottonseed, soybean seed and other seeds in oil, may be delighted, if asked, to let you cart away the organic residue left after the oil has been pressed out of the seeds (you might even be doing them a favor because in many cases disposal is a costly problem). Some towns sell and some give away sewage sludge. Find out what you can get where (free is best) and get whatever you can for your garden.

For phosphorous-rich fertilizers ask your favorite garden supply man for bone meal or the finely ground phosphate rock. Other rock dusts and powders such as granite and potash can be used to add the important potassium ingredient to your soil. Hardwood ashes, straight from your fireplace, if you are lucky enough to have one, can also be used as a potassium supply.

Other organic materials like sawdust, wood chips and straw can also be added to the soil, but they tend to take nitrogen from the soil when they decompose so use them sparingly.

Last, but far from least, of the organic soil additives is the frequently referred to organic gardener's favorite—compost. The reasons gardeners love this decayed organic material (which is really all that it is) are because it is natural, it is easily available, it is ecologically sound, it returns to nature after taking from nature and it is free. It produces marvelous humus which conditions and enriches your soil and solves the garbage disposal problem at the same time.

To make a compost heap, collect all the organic matter you can find and dump it somewhere toward the back of your property. Do not include cloth, bones, wood or meat scraps . . . these can be more trouble than they are worth. On a plot of bare ground (about four feet by four feet is a good size for most homeowners), lay about six inches of your best assorted organic waste materials. Supplement this with all the stuff you can beg or borrow from lumber yards (sawdust), supermarkets (spoiled produce) and factories (such throw-aways as shells and hulls from seeds and nuts, spent hops, grapes and others) and anything else organic. Try to see that each individual piece of waste is as small as possible. If everything is an inch or less you'll have fine, quick compost.

Drive several poles or posts into the ground through this first layer and continue to build your pile. Add a three- or four-inch layer of manure (from animal or poultry farms, or if need be, the garden supply store) and then a two- or three-inch layer of good soil, some wood ashes (preferably hardwood), some lime and any rock powders you find at the garden store. Water these layers . . . that is, wet them thoroughly but don't soak them. Then start all over. First the assorted "garbage," then the manure, then the topsoil, ashes and rock powder. Build the pile until it reaches a height of about four feet. Then pull out the stakes leaving aeration holes. About a month after your pile is complete, turn it with a spade or a fork, water and allow to stand for several additional weeks. Then, turn the pile again. In about three to four months you will have the most beautiful humus imaginable. In case you never thought you would consider humus a thing of beauty, work on a compost heap for months and months and see if, when the job is done, you don't agree.

Spread large amounts of this humus or compost on the area you selected for your garden and turn it, along with other not yet decomposed organic materials, into the soil.

Small areas can be turned over (turned under, or turned in, whichever you prefer to call it) with a spade or fork. Large areas should be done with a motor-powered plow or tiller. The size of the area, large versus small, is often determined as you stand at one edge and contemplate the amount of soil that must be turned under, one clod at a time. When you have decided that renting a tiller is best for your garden and your back, convince yourself that you will definitely make use of this large garden area.

Purists should dig down six to eight inches with their spade or fork, lift out a soil clod, turn it over so top is bottom and bottom is top and drop it back into place. Continue this process until the entire area has been turned under and you are questioning the sanity of your decision to garden. Remember to turn under compost, weeds, leaves, manure and other organic matter as you build up your soil (actually the soil then builds itself up without any more of your help) and condition it for spring planting.

Gardeners with weaker backs and larger gardens do basically the same job, but they do it with the help of a motorized plow or

*Large garden areas are best turned under by power tillers which
break up the soil and pulverize it while adding organic materials.*

tiller. A word of caution: Tillers are powerful, heavy pieces of
equipment. They can cause serious injuries if used carelessly or
improperly . . . especially when used by people like you and me
who are not accustomed to handling or working with equipment
of this type. So, when you use something like a tiller, pay strict
attention to the instructions and to the job at hand. Don't allow
yourself to be distracted. If there are young children in your
family, be sure that they are safely out of the way so you have no
fear of their being hit by a flying rock or of their distracting you
in any way.

When you have turned under the entire area you planned for your garden, there is really no other great physical work you need do until spring. Don't bother to rake out the lumps or smooth out the furrows. Leave everything just as it is and nature, in the form of sun, wind, rain and snow will do the job.

The last thing you want to do in the fall, before you hang up your gardening gloves for the season, is to collect some soil samples for testing. At this time, after a growing season, the nutrient level of your soil is as close to "normal" as it can be. The purpose of the test is to determine the soil's pH or acidity level. Most vegetables grow best in a slightly acid soil, so if you are above or below a pH level of about 6.0 (7.0 is neutral, 5.0 is very acidy) you should do something to correct the condition.

Very small amounts of soil are needed to do an accurate test, so put away your spade and do your collecting with a teaspoon. Take samples from various parts of your garden. All you really need is a teaspoonful. Put them into separate plastic bags, paper sacks or even into plastic or glass jars and send to your nearest county agent or state agriculture experiment station or cooperative extension service. In a very short time you will receive the results along with suggestions for correcting your acidity level.

If your soil tests out to be too sour, add ground or dolomitic limestone. If it tests out too sweet, adding wood ashes or sulphur will bring up the acidity.

Once your soil has been brought up to the proper pH you can retire from the physical side of gardening and go on to the mental pleasures of reminiscing, remembering and, of course, planning for next year. The new seed catalogs usually arrive in the dead of winter and there we all sit drooling over the gorgeous color pictures and trying to decide what to pick for next year. There is always a generous amount of: "Let's get more of this or . . . I hate that or . . . how about trying this this year or . . . no, that takes up too much room." But after a while things settle down, decisions are made, plans are drawn up and orders are written. Once you have decided, get that order into the mail immediately. Letting the order lie around will do you no good (orders don't ripen and get sweeter from lying around) and might in some instances mean that the particular variety you want may be out of stock by the time your order gets there. Good gardeners get their orders in early, like in January; not so efficient gardeners in

February; and the rest of us take potluck off the rack in our local garden shop in April, May or June.

With your order processed and now in your hands, you can actually begin working on your garden. In most parts of the country this includes starting seeds indoors so you can put healthy, sturdy seedlings into the ground at the proper time. Though there must be more, the main reasons given for starting seeds indoors include: Some plants (like celery) do not do well when started from seed sown directly into the soil; it lengthens the growing season and gives slower growers a bit of a head start; and, perhaps as important, it allows gardeners to "do something" while the ground is still covered with snow. The plants that do very well when started from seed indoors and then transplanted outdoors at the proper time include broccoli, Brussels sprouts, cabbage, cauliflower, cucumber, eggplant, lettuce, pepper, melon, tomatoes and herbs. Some, like squash, pumpkin and others also do well started indoors, but they do as well when started from seed directly in the ground.

The following step-by-step procedure has been found best for turning seeds into seedlings and then into strong, vigorous vegetable plants.

1. Start sowing your seeds indoors about eight weeks before they are due to be transplanted outdoors. Figure backward from the last day experts expect frost in your area, then add a safety factor.

2. Fill any of a wide variety of containers about half-way with a mixture of equal parts of sphagnum peat moss, sand and potting soil. If you do not want to mix your own, you can buy "seed-starting soil" at most garden supply stores. Containers are available in the form of seed flats, plant bands, peat pots, fiberboard flats and many others. If you prefer recycling and enjoy saving a few dollars, you can start seeds in coffee cans, egg cartons and milk and coffee containers.

3. Whatever method you use to obtain your seeds, be certain they are fresh and packed by a reputable company. Seed is quite inexpensive, so don't be penny-wise. Pay a few cents more for well-known, brand name fresh seed and you will be certain of quality and variety when planting.

Furrows pressed into seed-flat soil hold the seeds at the proper depth and distance for later transplanting.

4. Wet the soil in your container and let it stand a while so it becomes thoroughly soaked, but the excess water drains off. Using a dowel, stick or pencil, make furrows, the long way down the container, in the wet soil. Simply press the dowel into the soil, the flat way, lift off, and you have an instant furrow.

5. Hand-sow seed into the furrow. Space carefully according to the directions on the seed packet. Do not place too close together—healthier, sturdier seedlings come from correctly spaced seeds.

6. Cover the seeds with some of the same soil mixture you are using to hold the seeds. A very thin layer of soil will suffice. Water the covering layer of soil, but do it carefully and gently. Splashing lots of water around may wash your carefully planted seeds out of position.

A plastic bag placed over a seed flat becomes a miniature greenhouse and promotes even, full germination.

7. Slip the container (just as you have planted it) into a plastic bag. Bags used to store foods and those used for broiling will do just fine. Reuse plastic bags from the dry cleaners by knotting one end, placing the seed container inside and then knotting the other end. This is much cheaper and much better ecologically than buying new plastic bags. Encased in plastic, the seed flat will germinate more quickly and evenly because the plastic holds in moisture and softens light rays.

8. Position your miniature greenhouse in a warm (not hot), sunlit (indirect sunlight is preferable) spot, and allow it to remain there until germination of most of the seeds occurs. For best results keep the plastic-enclosed container in a spot that is uniformly warm and in filtered or soft sunlight for about six hours each day.

9. Watching and waiting comes next. Keep your eyes on the flats but do nothing but wait. After the seeds germinate, turn the flats 90° each day so the seedlings don't lean permanently towards the sun. When the first true leaves appear (these are the second set of leaves; the first ones look like the leaves on the mature plant, only smaller), carefully transplant the seedlings into individual peat pots, flats or any other individual pots.

The trick here is to get the seedlings out of the large flat and into the individual units without damaging or killing them. To do this you need some water, a dibble and a steady hand.

When your plants are ready for transplanting, fill the larger, individual pots (or whatever you are transplanting into) about half-way up with the same potting mixture you used to start the seeds, and prepare a hole for the seedling. Sprinkle water on the soil in the flat that still contains the seedlings. Carefully push a dibble (sounds terribly professional, doesn't it) or a pencil with a point, into the soil at about a 45° angle about one inch from the seedling you wish to remove. The angle of the dibble is important. The idea is to angle the dibble so it enters the soil about an inch away from the seedling and continues until it is under the seedling's roots. When the dibble is in place, gently hold the seedling between your thumb and forefinger and pop it out of the soil by pressing on the dibble.

Put the seedling into the hole you prepared for it in the new pot. The seedling should go down into the potting mixture as far as its first leaves, but not as far as its true leaves. Then it's back to the sunny window for a while. Continue to turn and to water these seedlings.

A week or two before you plan to move the seedlings into the garden, prepare them to meet the challenges of the great outdoors. Called hardening off, the process consists of withholding almost all water and placing the seedlings into a cold frame or other protected spot outdoors. If this toughening process is not accomplished, and the seedlings remain indoors in a sunny window until they are to be transplanted outside, they will be stringy, weak and less able to survive the temperature changes in the garden.

The last transplanting job is probably the most rewarding of all. This is the one that counts. All the work, all the watching, all

A dibble or pointed pencil is used to get under a seedling and pop it out so it may be transplanted to a larger container.

Cold frames help toughen tender seedlings and prepare them for the growing conditions that exist in the open garden.

the waiting and all the tender loving care pay off when you finally transplant your seedlings into their planned place in the garden.

Transplant only the sturdiest, healthiest looking seedlings. Less than perfect seedlings will probably not survive their first few weeks outside. There are two distinct transplanting methods, based upon the type of container in which the seedlings are growing. Flat-grown seedlings (and this includes those from commercial nurseries where they are planted twelve to a pack) require blocking, while individually grown seedlings are ready to go into the ground just as they are.

About ten days before you are ready to put your flat-grown seedlings into the ground, "block" or cut through the soil and the roots of each plant. Using a sharp knife, cut into the soil as you would into a brownie cake loaf. Cutting first in one direction and then in the other will result in individual cubes, each containing one plant, soil and roots. Make each cube as large as possible so as many roots and as much soil as possible are included with each cube.

Individual plants, plants started in growing cubes and plants growing in individual peat pots, can be planted pot and all. It is a good idea to thoroughly wet the plant, the soil and the organic pot just before planting. Whether or not your seedlings are blocked or in individual pots, do all transplanting on cloudy days or wait until the sun has gone down on a sunny day. Hot, steady sunlight may dry up and possibly kill delicate seedlings.

Use a taut string as a guide to dig the holes for all seedlings to be planted in a straight row. Dig all the holes deep enough and wide enough to accept seedling, soil and roots intact. Seedlings should be planted so the top of the root ball is just a bit below the surface of the garden soil. Tulip bulb planters make excellent hole makers for most seedlings.

After all the holes have been dug, place a small handful of composted material or dehydrated cow manure into each hole. If this is a two man, or one man and one woman job in your family, with the male digging the holes and the female setting the seedling into place, remind the manure thrower to be very careful on windy days and have pity on the seedling setter down there on the ground. When all holes are dug, place the seedlings into the holes. Water the plants thoroughly as they stand in the hole, but don't drown them. When the excess water has drained off,

Sturdy, healthy seedlings are knocked out of their containers so that plant, roots and soil are complete and will go into the garden as a unit.

Seedlings grown in organic pots are planted, pots and all. Tulip bulb planter makes hole in plastic mulch and soil at same time.

replace the soil all around the seedling. Carefully work some of the soil around the roots with your fingers. Don't pack it in tight, but tamp it down firmly so there are no air spaces left around the roots. Water again and let the soil and the water settle. Add soil as required, then make a slight depression all around the seedlings to catch rainwater.

If there is any doubt in your mind about the weather, especially the possible onset of a cold night, protect your newly planted seedlings either with fruit baskets, commercially available hot caps, tin cans or small pointed hats made from several sheets of newspaper. As soon as the weather has settled you may remove the protectors and allow the plants to make it on their own.

These general instructions apply to just about all vegetables. Specific information and instructions on individual vegetables are coming right up.

CHAPTER 2

None
Better Vegetables

IT WOULD SEEM, to the uninitiated, that "your troubles are over" when you see your seeds and seedlings thriving in the garden. To a certain extent that's true. Some of your troubles are over, but others are rapidly springing up to take their place. The soil that grows beautiful plants also grows huge weeds. The plants that are now bursting with obvious good health attract ruinous diseases. The vegetables that make your mouth water with their beauty and succulence have the same effect on a wide variety of insects and pests.

To some people the appearance of weeds, diseases and insects in the garden signals the start of an all-out war. They buy all the latest weapons—sprayers, dusters, foggers—and a fantastic assortment of "cides"—miticides, fungicides, herbicides, insecticides—and the battle is on. Without sounding too philosophical, this war is no different than any other . . . no one wins and everyone loses. The "cides" do their job, often too well, killing or ruining much more than you expected. That's bad enough, but what is worse is that the killing lingers on. You may have won the battle, but you've lost the war. Who wants to eat vegetables, fruits and berries covered with a poisonous spray? How can you be sure that your children or your neighbor's child will not succumb to the age-old temptation of eating a piece of ripe fruit picked right from the tree or bush? And, even when you yourself pick and wash the fruits and berries before serving them, can you really be sure that all the poisonous spray has been washed away?

Part of the answer to weed, insect and disease control lies in good gardening. The rest of the answer can be found in gardening's equivalent of preventative maintenance and in lavish doses of watchfulness and TLC.

Take weeding for example. Though many weeds are easily as pretty as other "regular" plants, they are not what you want and not what you planted, so you must get rid of them. Also, weeds growing right next to vegetables can't help but rob the vegetables of important nutrients and water. To keep a garden weed free you could spend most of your summer on your hands and knees pulling weeds. This is done several times a week for several hours each time. Some fun.

To our way of thinking, there has to be a better way and the magic word is mulch. If this is a new word in your vocabulary, do yourself a favor and learn it fast. This is a real old-time gardening favorite and does several jobs and not only does them well but does them at little or no cost. Simply stated, mulching consists of covering the areas around plants with readily available materials (mulches) which block out the weeds. The weeds cannot get through the layer of mulch and you save yourself a lot of backbreaking labor. Some of the best mulches are also the cheapest ones (costing nothing) such as leaves, grass clippings, straw, hay, ground corncobs, sawdust, pine needles, tree bark and many more. These and other mulches such as peat moss and cocoa bean hulls, and others you can buy, are all organic and return added value to the soil when plowed under after the growing season. They also continuously add nutrients to the soil during the growing season because they begin to decompose into the soil even while mulching your vegetables. Other materials which can be used as mulches but should not be plowed under (they don't decompose) include aluminum foil, gravel, stones and pebbles, fabric scraps and sheeted black plastic.

In addition to virtually eliminating the weed problem, mulches also help retain moisture in the soil, help regulate and maintain even soil temperatures and keep vegetables off the ground and out of water puddles. The man-made mulches like black plastic, newspapers and aluminum foil are put into place just before the seeds or seedlings are put into the ground. For best results, put the mulch into position, anchor it with sticks, stones or soil (dig a shallow trench on either side of the mulch sheets), lay in the mulch and hold it down by covering it with the scooped-out soil. Punch holes in the mulch to make room for the seeds or seedlings. Then plant.

The other or "spreadable" mulches should be put into place immediately after seedlings have been planted. Water the area thoroughly, put down a thick layer of mulch all around the seedlings and water the area again. Though a thick layer of mulch is far more effective than a very thin layer, too thick a layer can cause problems because light rains and waterings cannot penetrate to the soil. Mulches like leaves, straw, hay and grass clippings should be put down in three- to four-inch-thick layers. Peat moss, cocoa bean hulls and other "heavy" mulches will do the best job when put down about two inches thick.

If the idea of mulching to prevent weeds does not appeal to you, and you prefer to cultivate, good luck. A few words of friendly advice, though, if your back is killing you by the time you struggle through to the bitter end: grit your teeth, smile through your pain and repeat aloud, "Next time I'll mulch."

Back to cultivating. If you prefer the long-handled cultivators to the others which require you to crawl along between the rows on your hands and knees, be very careful of the depth of cultivation. Just break up the surface soil around the plants—cultivating too deeply can sever roots and severely damage or kill vegetable plants. Be especially careful about errant or "one last" swings with your cultivator—one wrong swing can cut a young plant in two.

Watering and fertilizing are important to the well-being of young and bearing plants. Though specific recommendations are included with the vegetable listing that follows, some general suggestions are pertinent here. First and most important, plants must have a considerable amount of water every week if they are to produce beautiful vegetables. It is not enough to depend on rainwater (except in areas where it rains several times each week during the summer), nor is it enough to sprinkle the ground around your plants every day and consider them watered.

When you water, WATER, do not tease the plants. To check

on whether your garden is getting the inch of water it needs every week, place a few empty coffee cans around the garden and use them to measure the amount of rainfall and the amount of your watering. Always water thoroughly, but don't drown the plants. If at all possible water during that part of the day when the sun starts down (watering during the hottest part of the day results in water loss due to evaporation which is both inefficient and extravagant). But don't wait to water too late in the day. Allow enough time for the leaves to dry before nightfall (to prevent fungi and diseases from getting a foothold).

Fertilizing should also be accomplished according to a plan and not on a hit-or-miss basis. Too many gardeners are not careful about their timing or amount of fertilizer. Often they feel that if a little fertilizer is good, a lot is even better. Of course nothing could be further from the truth. Unless small, correct amounts of fertilizer are used, and used at the right times, you will probably produce plants with lots of leaves and no vegetables; plants that grow to giant size and cannot support their growth and weight, and most likely, dead plants.

For a simple, effective fertilizing schedule, assume first that you mixed organic fertilizer with your garden soil as you prepared the area for planting. When you are actually ready to plant, place a little composted fertilizer in each planting hole before putting in the seed or seedling. Do nothing until the plant is about one foot tall; then put some more of the composted organic matter two or three inches away from the stem, in a ring around the stem. Fertilize for the last time when the flowers have gone and the vegetables are starting to grow. Once again a ring of organic fertilizer several inches away from the plant's stem will do the trick. Do not use chemical fertilizers—most are too strong and will usually burn the plants on contact and often severely damage or kill them.

The subject of killing or damaging plants brings us to the problems caused by insects and diseases in the garden. These are real problems, but they are not insurmountable and they can be solved without having to resort to the use of sprays and poisons. Perhaps the most important item of garden housekeeping, and one which will most greatly reduce the insect and disease problem is that of the cleanliness of the garden. Diseases, fungi and insects breed and multiply in wetness, in filth and in unhealthy plants.

Sheeted black plastic serves as a mulch for developing vegetable plants. Grass clippings between the rows virtually eliminate all weeding.

If you do nothing else to prevent disease in your garden, at least keep your garden as clean as possible and your plants as healthy as possible. Get rid of all leaves, fruits, vegetables and other debris. If this kind of organic material is not diseased, toss it on the compost heap. If anything is diseased, burn it or put it out with the trash. Check your organic mulches. Make sure they are not in position so long they have decayed and become insect breeding grounds. At the end of each growing season plow under the organic mulches (or compost them) and start out fresh the next season.

When you do your planning you can actually plan out many garden insects and diseases. Always rotate your crops. Never plant the same vegetables in the same part of the garden year after year. In one area put root crops one year and leaf crops the next. Keep mixing, changing and moving . . . keep the insects off balance. Large expanses of a single kind of planting are an open invitation to insects and diseases that thrive on that specific vegetable. Plant your rows far enough apart so air can circulate, leaves can dry and diseases have a harder time getting started. Take a good, long look at your drainage situation, too. Plants allowed to sit in puddles of water for long periods of time will frequently fall prey to a wide variety of diseases and a great many different insects.

Carefully examine vegetables, plant leaves and all the areas on the ground around the plant for the telltale signs of trouble. Curled leaves, spots, holes, color changes, insect droppings, eggs and anything else out of the ordinary indicate trouble. Being aware of trouble is about half the battle. The other half is finding the correct answer to the particular problem. Your aim is to keep the pests from ruining your produce, not to completely eradicate all insects. There is much to be said about nature's balance, but sometimes you must take action to protect your investment in time, money and labor.

Start out by using a strong water-only spray to knock insects from your plants. You can then either step on them or leave them to their natural enemies (more about that later) as they lie stunned on the ground. Those who are not taken care of in either of these two ways will probably be right back to do their dirty work the very next day. The next step would be to try spraying your plants with a soapy water (not detergents). Ever taste soapy water? Insects don't like it either. Handpicking and then "getting rid" of them can work for large devastators including the big, ugly, tomato hornworm.

There's another group of sprays that can be used in the garden without any fear, except for the odor they exude. (The entire garden tends to smell like a crowded subway train during rush hour.) Mix any of the following—onion, garlic, marigold, pepper or tobacco—with an equal amount of water in an electric blender. Liquefy the mixture, pass it through a sieve and spray the liquid on your garden plants. Most bugs will develop such a heartburn they'll never come near your garden again. How you explain the pungent aroma to your neighbors is another story and your problem.

One last group of sprays also rates investigation. These substances are extracted from plants and are called botanicals. Despite the name they are only "relatively safe" and should be used only as a last resort when all other methods fail. Though

By keeping rows of vegetables several feet apart you limit the number and kinds of insects and diseases likely to attack your plants.

The aroma given off by onion sets will keep many flies and other pests from your produce. These and other natural controls are very effective and should be experimented with.

these natural insecticides, including rotenone and pyrethrin, are harmless to all warm-blooded creatures (man and pets), they are harmful to fish and should not be used near streams or other fish-filled areas.

Natural controls take other forms which are easily as effective. One of these programs suggests that you plant certain plants near other plants to keep specific insects at bay. For example, garlic planted near the base of peach trees is supposed to keep the peach tree borer away. Chives planted around rose bushes keeps the rose bushes aphid free. Carrot flies and cabbage loopers steer clear of rows planted with herbs including mint, sage and rosemary. Horseradish will banish potato bugs while asparagus takes care of tomato worms. Also, onion sets (not seeds) will send out a natural aroma repugnant to carrot flies and onion flies. There are other plants that control destructive bugs on your vegetable plants, but the ones just mentioned are the most widely used and do the best job on the greatest number of pests.

The other natural control program, the one we like the best, uses beneficial insects and birds to do their "own thing." We have watched ladybugs clean off a rose bud infested with aphids in a remarkably short time. Ladybugs, praying mantises, lace-wings and trichogramma wasps are our favorite garden compan-ions. They get out into the garden early, they work late, don't take long coffee breaks or vacations and never seem to get tired of doing their thing which, in this case, is destroying insects which we consider harmful. If you didn't know, you can purchase these insects from local nurseries or through the mail. Release them in the garden as directed and watch the incredible results.

Birds, too, can be a great help in ridding your garden of insect pests and they are even cheaper than the store bought insects. Matter of fact, most birds will work for peanuts, or a little suet or birdseed. Set up a feeder, birdhouse or birdbath near the garden, keep them filled and you will have a devoted crew of allies as you battle nature's destroyers. If you keep these birdfeeders filled all winter, the birds will get into the habit of coming to your property for food and will then return every year during warm weather to continue feeding.

Do a little experimenting on your own with your own "home-grown" remedies and deterrents and you may find still more combinations that will work best for you and save the largest amount of vegetables from your garden. A few vegetables lost to insects is not such a big deal compared to the mounting catastrophe that spraying with poisons (to eradicate all insects) causes. Just try to keep the insects as far away as possible without killing unnecessarily and all will be right with the world.

ASPARAGUS—If your family likes them, plant them. Fresh asparagus are a delicacy not easily found in local vegetable stores and supermarkets.

Though asparagus can be grown from seed, your best bet is to pay a little bit more and put in one-year-old plants that have at least a twelve-inch-long root spread. Matter of fact, in this case, the longer the better. They're very economical—some plantings yield delicious, tender stalks for as many as fifty years.

Best time to plant asparagus crowns is early spring, shortly after the garden has been carefully prepared. Select a spot for your asparagus and other perennials (they come back each year) at one end of the garden where they will not have to be moved. Dig a trench that's at least one and one-half feet wide and one and one-half feet deep. Shovel back into the trench about one foot of rotted manure, compost, rotted leaves or other organic materials. When the bottom of the trench has been filled up to six inches below the "normal" soil level, start putting the asparagus crowns into place. Place the crowns about eighteen inches apart and spread their roots out in the trench. Hold in position while you cover with about one inch of soil. Use the remaining soil, little by little, by working it around the plants all during the first season they are in the ground. Water thoroughly, but do not drown.

Mary Washington, Martha Washington and Waltham Washington are excellent asparagus varieties, with Mary and Martha especially good for freezing. Do not try to grow asparagus in those parts of the country that remain warm all through the winter. Asparagus do best in those areas where winter temperatures drop low enough for the top two inches of soil to become frozen. Results are spindly and disappointing in other areas.

BEANS—Almost anyone can grow and enjoy all sorts of beans—snap, pole and lima. All need reasonably well-fertilized soil that is light-textured. Heavy soils tend to bake and become hard, preventing the seed sown seedlings from breaking through the soil crust.

Prepare soil in early spring but wait until all danger of frost has passed before planting. Use fresh seed that has been soaked overnight in cool water to hasten germination. Then sow directly into the garden in rows about three feet apart. Seed should be placed about one inch deep and three inches apart. Cover with loose soil and water thoroughly. Vine-type beans like pole beans require some sort of support on which to climb. Do not use lumberyard-cut boards as stakes because their smoothness and angularity are difficult for the vine's tendrils to grasp and climb. Mesh netting, rough-hewn saplings or several taut strings make excellent climbing supports.

Some of the best varieties include Tender Pod and Topcrop (bush beans), Pencil Pod and Surecrop (wax beans), Kentucky Wonder (snap pole beans), Fordhook 242 (bush lima beans) and Challenger and King of the Garden (large-seeded pole lima beans). All of the mentioned varieties freeze well.

In some areas of the country successive plantings can be made at two-week intervals all spring and summer or at least until about eight weeks before the first killing frost.

When working among bean plants—for weeding, cultivating or picking—avoid touching the plants when their leaves are wet. If any diseases are present they will, in all probability, be spread from one plant to another by touching the wet leaves.

BEETS—Keep a few "basics" in mind and you'll have great success with this beautiful, tasty root crop. First, they can be grown in just about every part of the country, but they grow best in cool rather than extremely hot weather. Second, beets prefer soil that is not too acidy, so dig in enough natural limestone to move the pH balance up closer to neutral. Third, and this goes for all root crops, keep the soil loose and easily breakable. Seedlings will quickly die if the soil cakes and hardens and doesn't allow the fragile seedlings to break through the surface.

Plant beets in rows about eighteen inches apart and one inch deep after adding manure to the soil. When seeds have sprouted and are six inches tall, thin the beets so the individual plants are about three inches apart. Each beet "seed" planted contains three or four real seeds so expect to get a considerable amount of young tender beet greens for early spring salads. For home garden planting, Crosby Egyptian, Detroit Dark Red and Early Wonder are the recommended varieties.

CABBAGE FAMILY—A very popular and important crop in the home garden, this family includes broccoli, Brussels sprouts, cauliflower and, of course, cabbage. Each can be grown in every part of the United States, but each also has a definite weather preference. Broccoli does best in cool temperature areas; Brussels sprouts can tolerate even colder weather; cabbage will do well in all but the hottest parts of the country; and cauliflower, though hardy, can stand neither the same amount of cold as cabbage, nor excessive heat (in which it will not head).

All cabbage family members grow best in soils rich in organic matter and not too acidy. Though all can be grown in the garden from seed, it is a much better idea to sow the seed indoors and plant six- to eight-week-old plants in the garden. A handful of composted or dehydrated cow manure, dropped in the hole at planting time, gets the plants off to a good start. As the plants develop, keep them evenly watered. If they should be denied water for a while and then given it again, the heads will most probably split.

Space the plants for all cabbage family members about eighteen inches apart in rows about thirty inches apart. Plant these vegetables deeper in the ground than most other vegetables to give a bit more support to their top-heavy heads. Recommended varieties for broccoli are Calabrese, Green Sprouting and Waltham 29; for Brussels sprouts, Long Island Improved and Jade Cross; for cabbage, Golden Acre, Copenhagen Market and Red Acre (red) are early types, and Danish Ballhead and Wisconsin Hollander are later types; and for cauliflower, Early Snowball, Snowball and Perfection.

CARROTS—These vitamin-rich vegetables can grow almost anywhere at any time, but they must have rock-free, loose, loamy soil if they are to reach their peak in looks and taste. Carrots grown in rocky, lumpy soil become tough and misshapen. Soil just a bit on the sandy side gives the best results.

Plant carrots in rows about eighteen inches apart and no more than one-half-inch deep. It's a good idea to put a few radish seeds in with the carrot seeds to mark the row (carrots take a lot longer than radishes to come up) and to break through the soil if a crust has formed. When the plants are about six inches tall, thin to two inches between each plant. A carefully placed layer of mulch on each side of the carrot row will help keep moisture in the soil and keep the carrots growing evenly.

Recommended carrot varieties include Tendersweet, Danvers Half Long, Nantes, Imperator and Chantaney.

CORN—This primarily warm-weather crop can be grown in most parts of the United States if the seed is put into the ground early enough, but not before the soil has been thoroughly warmed. Whatever effort must go into this vegetable is more than repaid by the first bit of "right off the stalk, home-grown" corn.

Almost any soil will do for corn, but because it is wind pollinated, it must be planted in several short rows placed side by side rather than in a single long row. Sow seed directly into the ground either in rows (drills) or in hills. When sown in drills drop one corn seed about one inch deep every six inches in rows that are three feet apart. When planting in hills drop several (six or seven) seeds in each hill. Keep hills three feet away from each other. Thin drill-sown corn until you have plants every foot and thin hill-sown seed until only three or four remain in each hill. Supply large amounts of water to plants unless you have enough rain. Because corn should be eaten immediately after removal from the stalk and there's only so much corn a family can eat, make several successive sowings about ten days apart. This will give you fresh, sweet, wonderful corn, seconds from the stalk, for a longer period of time. Though it's not as good as fresh, frozen corn is a fine treat on a cold winter day.

Very often corn earworms ruin an entire crop just as it reaches maturity. To keep these worms from getting to your corn before you do, use an eyedropper to drip a few drops of castor or mineral oil on the silks just as they turn brown. It takes time and can become tedious, but it can very well mean the difference between a mouth-watering taste treat for you or your local corn earworms.

Some exceptionally fine tasting corn varieties include North Star, Golden Bantam, Golden Cross Bantam, Surecross, Honeycross and Country Gentlemen.

CUCUMBER—Good fertile soil, warm weather and lots of water are the recipe for growing large quantities of crisp, tasty

Trained to grow up a turkey wire trellis, these cucumbers will have a high yield, with little or no loss, and take up as little space as most bush plants.

cukes. Whether you plant seed or seedlings, wait until all danger of frost is past before you do any cucumber planting. The best way to plant these vines is in hills, that is, several seeds sown in a single small area with the vines allowed to grow outward from this central point. Though you can sow seed directly in the ground for cucumbers, you get a valuable head start when you start the seeds indoors and set them out in the garden as seedlings. Thin the plants in each hill to two or three and make sure each hill is at least six feet away from the nearest hill.

Because they are vines and require considerable amounts of space when allowed to roam on their own over the garden, many gardeners feel other crops are more suitable to the small home garden. If space is your problem you can grow cucumbers, but don't let them roam. Simply train them to grow up a wooden or turkey wire trellis and you can have your cukes and space, too.

Good varieties for pickling include SMR 12 and Chicago Pickling. For slicing, your best bet is Burpee Hybrid or Smoothie. If your mind says yes but your stomach says no, try one of the "Burpless" varieties currently being offered by the larger seed merchants.

EGGPLANT—These warm weather beauties require very little space and good soil to produce large, firm, delicious fruits. Plants should be started indoors, hardened off for a week or two in a cold frame and transplanted to the garden when all danger of frost is gone and the soil has been thoroughly warmed. Put seedlings into the garden so they are about thirty inches each way from other eggplants. Consistent watering is more important than the quantity of water if the plants are to produce excellent fruits. A mulch of straw or hay all around the plants will help keep the soil temperature steady, keep moisture in the ground and provide a cushion or base upon which the fruits can lie, keeping them out of the soil and water.

Two favorite varieties for home gardens are Black Beauty and New Hampshire Hybrid.

LETTUCE—The many different varieties of this popular salad vegetable make it easy for most home gardeners to find a favorite. Primarily a cool weather crop, lettuce will go to seed (bolt) at the first signs of hot, dry weather. For this reason it is wiser to choose a leaf lettuce variety than a head lettuce variety in those areas where hot weather comes early in the season.

Leaf lettuce seed can be planted directly in the garden as early in the spring as the soil is workable. Sow the seed in rows two feet apart and thin as required. The very young leaves removed from the rows make excellent salad greens. Head lettuce varieties should be started indoors and then transplanted to the garden very early in the spring. Put the plants into rows that are about two feet apart with each head of lettuce about eighteen inches away from the next head in the row. Use a mulch around each head to keep it clean and off the ground. Keep all lettuce well watered and free of weeds.

Best varieties of leaf lettuce for the home garden include Salad Bowl, Grand Rapids and Slobolt. For head lettuce choose either White Boston, Iceberg, Imperial 456 or Great Lakes.

ONION—Just a little bit of space, a lot of water and some mild temperatures and anyone can grow enough onions for an entire family for a year. Grown from seed, sets (small, dry onions grown the previous year) and seedlings, onions are easily grown in almost any soil that is rich in fertilizer and crumbly to the touch. Home gardeners do best when they start their onions from sets. Put the sets or seedlings into rows that are eighteen inches apart as early in the spring as the ground is workable. Space them so each onion is about three inches away from the next one. Keep them thoroughly watered and free from weeds.

When the tops get very large, turn yellow or start to set seed, bend them over to the ground, break them, but do not tear them off. By doing this you direct all of the plant's growing energy to the bulb, the part most of us eat.

There are many, many different kinds and varieties of onions so pick the ones you like the best. For example, if you like them on hamburgers, choose Bermuda or Granex; if you like them on the mild side, choose Sweet Spanish or Golden Beauty; and if you want to do some experimenting, try Italian Red, Ebenezer, Yellow Globe, Southport White Globe (or Red Globe if you prefer) and Abundance.

PEAS—Get these in the ground early in the spring because peas, unlike beans, are a cool-weather crop. Sow the seeds directly into the ground (after overnight soaking like beans) immediately after you have added large amounts of organic matter and checked to see that the soil is far from acidy. Scratch a furrow into the soil with a hoe and water the area thoroughly. Place the seed into the furrows (rows should be twenty-four inches apart) about one inch apart. Cover with loose soil and withhold any more water until the seedlings start to poke up through the soil. Thin plants to a two-inch spacing and start to water regularly again. Many pea varieties grow best when allowed to climb up a piece of string, some wire or a trellis, so provide one whenever possible. Recommended varieties for early peas include Lincoln, Little Marvel and World's Record. Good peas for later harvest include Freezonian and Thomas Laxton.

PEPPER—These plants are so pretty they can be used around the house for decoration with the extra added attraction of providing tasty sweet or hot peppers. Definitely hot weather plants, peppers are similar in culture to tomatoes, and though they enjoy steady moisture, they do not like to stand in water for any length of time.

Wait until all danger of frost is gone before sowing seed or putting out seedling plants. Planting sturdy seedling plants gives you a considerable jump toward quicker pepper picking. Space peppers about twenty inches apart in the row, with each row about two feet away from other rows. Use mulch around and between the plants to maintain moisture and eliminate weeding.

Some excellent sweet peppers are California Wonder, Ruby King, Vineland and Yale Wonder. For those who like their peppers hot there's Long Red Cayenne and Red Chili—either is a taste treat.

POTATO—Few people grow their own potatoes, but those that do sing their praises all year round. If you live in an area that only gets storage potatoes, give up the little extra space they require in the garden and grow some of your own.

For best results with your potato growing, start early. Work on the soil should begin in the fall for potato planting the following spring. If you can, grow a crop of rye grass or alfalfa the year before you want to put in your first potatoes. Then, just before you're ready to start work on the soil, plow the rye or alfalfa under—it will become excellent green manure, feeding the soil while adding generous amounts of organic matter.

Use only certified seed potatoes for planting. Do not use the same potatoes you buy in the supermarket for planting. They are for eating and seed potatoes are for planting. Cut the seed potatoes into block-shaped pieces (not wedges) with each piece having at least one and preferably two eyes. Do not plant the pieces too early, or the combination of long stretches of cold and wet weather could cause the potato pieces to rot.

Dig a six-inch-deep trench and place the potato pieces in it, cut-side down (eyes up), about eighteen inches apart. Cover until all but two inches of the trench has been refilled with soil. When the plants are about one foot tall, add the remaining soil to the trench making it level with the rest of the garden.

Potatoes like steady moisture, but do not do well if the soil is kept very wet. Mulch around the plants will help keep the moisture at a good, steady level. Some good early potato varieties are Irish Cobbler, Early Gem and Norlan. For excellent later potatoes select from Sebago, Russet Burbank, Green Mountain and Kennebec.

PUMPKIN—Only grow these big orange beauties if you have plenty of space to spare, for that's what they need. Follow the same planting procedure suggested for cucumbers except allow at least ten feet between seed hills. Also, note that pumpkin do well in partial shade, so if you have a spot, behind corn or another tall crop that's not suited to anything else, put in some pumpkin. Two recommended varieties for the home garden are Sugar and Jack O'Lantern.

RADISHES—Everybody grows radishes because everyone has success growing radishes. For you to be successful, all you need do is place the seed in the furrow at one-inch intervals early in the spring. Do your planting early as radishes do well in cool weather and very poorly in heat. Put in a few successive plantings and you'll have more than enough for the entire season. Remember that radishes mature about three weeks after planting, so pick and eat them as soon as possible or they get woody and bitter. Especially good varieties are Cherry Belle, Scarlet Globe and Icicle (white).

RHUBARB—Spade in the manure and you'll reap a bountiful, beautiful, succulent harvest. Almost anytime during fall and straight through spring can be used for planting the crowns or roots. (Rhubarb can be started from seed, but the roots are a far better, safer bet.) Set the crowns in hills four feet apart each way, mulch well (preferably with manure) and water well, but do not allow the plants to stand in water. This is a perennial so put it in a spot where it will not be disturbed. Feed well twice each season, spring and summer, and keep weed-free. Don't do any picking the first year, but after that a few plants will give you all the rhubarb you can eat and give away. Good varieties include Valentine, Cherry, Strawberry and Victoria.

SPINACH—These leaves do best in cool weather and non-acid, almost sandy soil. Sow seeds one inch deep as early in spring as the soil can be worked. When the leaves start coming up, thin to about four inches apart. Use the thinned leaves in salads or cooked, just as you would the more mature spinach leaves. Successive sowing in early spring and again in early fall will provide the best spinach you or Popeye ever tasted. While the spinach is growing, apply a light-side dressing of fertilizer and keep the water coming. Recommended varieties are Bloomsdale Long Standing, Virginia Savoy and America.

SQUASH—For the many, many varieties of squash, follow the same planting directions as given for cucumbers and pumpkins, only more so. Try out lots of them including the summer ones: pattypan, crookneck, cocozelle and zucchini and the winter offerings: corn, hubbard, butternut, banana and turban.

Tomatoes must be staked and trained to these stakes while they are still quite young. Keeping the tomatoes off the ground cuts down on losses to disease.

TOMATO—Be good to these American favorites and they will be good to you. Start tomato plants indoors six to eight weeks before you plan to set them into the garden—that's when all danger of frost is gone. Keep them about three feet each way from each other in well-fertilized and well-watered soil. Mulching around each plant will just about insure your getting a full, trouble-free crop. Pinch back all suckers and stake tomatoes or attach them to some sort of an A-frame or trellis. Though this kind of growing procedure may result in a slightly smaller crop, the tomatoes you get (and they'll still be abundant) will be clean, easy to find and pick and a lot less susceptible to many diseases, bugs and rotting.

There are so many wonderful tomato varieties from which to choose that recommendations are pointless. Select from all the disease- and wilt-resistant varieties and experiment by growing a plant or two of several kinds each year until you hit upon the variety that you like the best. Don't forget to grow the various types including cherry, plum, beefsteak and yellow along with your particular favorites.

HERBS—Take your pick and you can have whatever you want whenever you want it, either in your kitchen or out in the garden. Since it's almost impossible to list them all here, along with growing instructions (that's a whole new book), a few general comments. Most herbs can be started in small pots indoors and then either kept indoors and used when necessary or moved to the garden for even bigger and better growth. Indoors, keep them in a sunny window and water and feed them well. Outdoors, put them into well-fertilized soil and watch them grow; then, when cool weather rolls around, get them back into pots and back inside for the winter. This can go on forever and you'll always have the freshest, most aromatic herbs and spices available anywhere.

After all, you're going to put these marvelous flavorings together with some pretty fine vegetables to produce some very good eating. So, plant enough fruits and vegetables for eating raw, eating cooked and either canning, freezing or preserving. Everything you do adds up to some wonderful experiences in the garden and in the kitchen.

CHAPTER 3

Pure and Simple Cooking

THERE'S NOT MUCH point in growing your own vegetables if you are going to ruin them in cooking. That's what most people do—they spend lots of time, money and effort growing unbeatable vegetables and then they cook them and cook them and cook them until they are tasteless, colorless, worthless lumps. The reason for this is simple. People become accustomed to cooking and preparing supermarket produce and forget that store bought and garden fresh are completely different kinds of vegetables. Everything about them is different.

The produce you buy in a supermarket or local vegetable store has been bred to withstand some of the rigors of modern life including mechanical harvesting, packing, shipping over long distances, and days and days in and out of refrigeration. Any wonder they're bred tough?

Want to prove it to yourself? Buy some corn on the cob at the supermarket. When you get it home, boil a pot of water. While the water boils, saunter to your garden, pick an ear of corn and run with this treasure back to your kitchen. Place both dehusked ears into the pot. Cook for about five minutes. Remove both from the water and slather on melted butter followed by salt and pepper to taste. Take a bite first from one ear, then from the other. One mouthful and you'll be sure which one came from your garden and which one came from the store. You'll also be sold forever on home gardening.

There is no comparison, no contest. Home-grown vegetables are something special and should be treated that way. And remember, this special handling includes cooking. The least cooking means the best-tasting vegetables.

Here are a few basic ideas for you to keep in mind when your vegetables are just about ready for picking: Check your garden every morning and pick whatever is ripe. Do not allow ripe vegetables to remain on the plant in the hope they will get bigger and better. They will get bigger but they won't get better. Usually along with bigness comes coarseness in taste and texture. And, while we are talking about the best, use only perfect vegetables in your cooking and serving. Holes, blemishes and bruises can sometimes be cut away and the vegetable used for cooking or sauce making, but the rule of thumb stands: Perfect vegetables make perfect meals.

One of the reasons home-grown vegetables taste so superior to store bought is the fact that chemical changes start in many vegetables almost immediately after they have been picked. To get the best-tasting vegetables, cook them as soon after they have been picked as possible. It may seem strange to your neighbors as they watch you dash madly from your garden to your house with an armload of produce, but don't worry. The taste of your from-garden-to-kitchen-stove vegetables will be proof enough of your sanity. If your neighbor has a garden, he will understand. If he doesn't, he will not and no amount of talking will convince him or make him understand.

There are times when this kind of immediate cooking is impossible. In these cases, wrap the vegetables in newspaper, paper toweling or waxed paper and store in your refrigerator crisper until they can be cooked.

When preparing vegetables for cooking, do as little to them as possible. If they have been kept free of sprays and dusts and all the available chemicals, they are ready to go. Wash them in cold water using a vegetable brush. Scrub them quickly, then dry. Do not soak vegetables in water to get them clean. Many vitamins and some of the taste will go down the drain with the wash water. Peel only those vegetables that you must, the rest leave whole. A great deal of nutrition in many vegetables is found just under the skin, so don't throw it away.

Eat as many vegetables as you can just as they come from the garden—raw. It's usually the best way. For many of us this is a matter of changing our way of thinking and the way we have become accustomed to eating vegetables. Put some variety into your life. Approach it as a new experience and give yourself a chance to try, test, taste and enjoy.

For those vegetables you must cook, a few suggestions: If water is needed to cook vegetables, use as little as possible. The more water you use the more diluted the natural taste becomes. Cook all vegetables only until they are done, but are still crisp. (Another unexpected experience you have to get used to.) It is usually better to undercook vegetables just a bit than to overcook them. Do not discard either the cooking water or the juices left in the pot after cooking. They are nutritious and tasty and can be used in gravies, soups and various dressings. The reason most recipes call for cooking in a covered saucepan is that the cover prevents considerable loss of vitamins through steam.

With these suggestions you will get the best taste and the best vegetables from your garden. Before you cook your vegetables, you need to know the best time and the right way to harvest them. Often this is a hard question to answer. You think the particular vegetable looks perfect and is right for picking, but you are not sure, and often it isn't. Here's how and when to harvest home-grown vegetables along with some basic cooking suggestions.

ASPARAGUS—This vegetable has been a favorite for well over 2,000 years and still is today. Start cutting firm stalks (only after asparagus have been in your garden three years) when they are ready, around the beginning of May. Continue to cut as they become ready for the next eight weeks. Use a sharp knife to cut the stalks slightly below the soil's surface when the stalks reach a height of six to eight inches. When the spears are allowed to grow taller they get spindly and are not nearly as good to eat. If you are afraid a sharp knife might damage the roots, you may simply snap off the spears with your fingers.

To cook, wash asparagus in cold water and eliminate any loose scales. Make a bundle of 10 to 12 spears, of the same thickness, using kitchen cord, and stand in about one inch of boiling, salted water. Cover and cook for eight to ten minutes. If you do not have a pot tall enough to accommodate standing asparagus, ad lib by using two pots, one right side up and the other upside down. Test asparagus stalk bottom with fork. It should be tender but not limp—crisp but not hard. Untie bundles and serve hot with butter or favorite sauce.

GREEN BEANS—Known under various names including snap bean and string bean (the yellow ones are called wax beans), this vegetable can be grown and picked all summer long. Start picking when beans are full but before seeds start making a bump in the pod. Pick as often as there are beans to be had. Sometimes this means at least once a day. Pick only when the plant's leaves are dry—wet leaves can transmit disease and ruin both plant and harvest.

Prepare the beans for cooking by snapping off the ends and then leaving whole (especially the thin, young ones) or snapping into bite-sized pieces. Drop beans into saucepan containing one and one-half inches of rapidly boiling, salted water. Allow to come back to boil, cover and cook for about 10 minutes. Test with fork. Beans should be crisp, not soft. You'll be surprised to discover that beans cooked properly need to be chewed before swallowing (as should all the vegetables from your garden).

LIMA BEANS—This very close relative to the string or green bean is eaten for its bean instead of its pod, so don't harvest these until the pods are fat and the beans show through the skin. Pick these beans when they are green—once they start to turn yellowish green they are deteriorating in taste and tenderness. Chemical changes take place in these beans soon after picking, so cook as soon after picking as possible for best taste.

Baby lima beans can be cooked pod and all. Simply dump them into a pot of boiling water and cook for about 30 minutes. Test by opening a pod and eating a bean. Larger lima beans should be shelled first, then dumped into one and one-half inches of boiling, salted water and cooked for between 25 and 30 minutes in a covered saucepan.

BEETS—Many people throw away the best part of this vegetable when they discard the green tops. These dark green leaves are not only delicious when prepared in the same way as spinach, but are an even richer source of iron, and they are available long after spinach has stopped growing. Try them. You'll be surprised at the taste.

Pull the beets out of the ground when they are one and one-half to two inches in diameter. Though some varieties grow even bigger, the premium in taste and tenderness comes when they are about two inches around or less.

Prepare your beets for cooking by washing in cold water and cutting off all but about one and one-half to two inches of the top. Do not peel or scrape the beets. Save the greens and cook as you would spinach. Boil enough water in a saucepan to cover the beets. Put in the beets, cover the pan and boil for about 18 minutes or until the beets are soft to the touch. Drain the water and slide off the skins. Then cut off the top stem and any small roots that remain and serve.

BROCCOLI—Another longtime vegetable favorite, broccoli is part of the cabbage family along with Brussels sprouts, cauliflower and the less popular kale and kohlrabi. Broccoli must be watched when it gets close to harvest time—or it will be too late before you know it.

Cut the heads while the buds are still shut tight and before any tiny yellow flowers appear. If there are yellow flowers on your broccoli, you've missed the perfect picking time. Cut the heads so that about six inches of stem remain with them. Later crops will come from shoots that grow after the first head has been cut. If you can't cook broccoli immediately after harvesting, keep it in a cool place with its stem in cold water until you can.

Basic broccoli cooking is quick and simple. Put the broccoli into a covered pot that contains about one and one-half inches of salted water that has been brought to a boil. Cook for about 10 to 12 minutes and check to see if the stalks are as tender and crisp as the floweret or head part. Drain and serve.

BRUSSELS SPROUTS—This cabbage relative looks like a cabbage that didn't make good. When the buds are a bit larger than a ping pong ball but smaller than a golf ball it is the perfect time for harvesting. Twist the buds from the stalk, trim and cook, that's all there is to it.

Cooking this vegetable is also quite simple. Remove the

outermost layer of leaves and put the pretty green bud into about one inch of salted, rapidly boiling water. Cover the saucepan and cook for no more than seven minutes. Drain and serve with or without butter or your favorite sauce.

CABBAGE—The head of this family is known and used in virtually every part of the world in a variety of sizes, colors and shapes. Harvest your cabbage when it has good color and good size, just before it starts to split. Check the variety to get an idea of the mature size of the head. Twist the entire plant while holding the stem and the head. Then, just lift when you feel it come free. Trim off stem and break off outer, tougher leaves. Hosing it down outdoors is a good idea and will often spare the possibility of an unexpected discovery of a small, crawly friend or two at the base of the head. Prepare as soon as possible according to your favorite recipe.

Remember that one of the tastiest ways to prepare and serve cabbage is raw. If you must cook it, do it carefully. Don't overcook it. Too much cooking and a slight breeze will result in quick alienation of neighbors and friends.

CARROTS—Everyone knows that carrots are good for your eyesight. But, how many know that the Vitamin A in carrots will help keep you young? Need any more reason to look at carrots in a different light? If you have planted them as early as soil conditions allow in your area, they will be ready for very early picking. Start pulling them in early July and pull only what you need. You can continue pulling them and enjoying them as long as they last.

Scrub the carrots with a vegetable brush but do not scrape with a scraper. Cook in one inch of boiling, salted water in a covered saucepan for about 10-15 minutes. Check by pushing a fork into one of the carrots. When it goes in with just a bit of pressure from you, your carrots are done to perfection. But, for the greatest treat of all, pick a carrot from the garden, wash under the hose and . . . enjoy.

CAULIFLOWER—This vegetable takes a little extra effort but the eating payoff is well worth the trouble. Because Americans prize cauliflower with a bleached white floweret, the leaves must be drawn up around the head soon after it becomes a head.

Keeping the heads completely shaded produces the white color. If you want to be adventurous, leave one head half shaded and the other half unshaded. You may be surprised at the results. For harvesting, wait about two to three weeks before making your leaf upsweep. The heads should be firm and beautifully full. Cut the head off where it meets the stem (about where head and leaves start) and trim the leaves so they are about one inch from the top of the head all around.

When you are ready for a vegetable treat, break the cauliflower apart into flowerets and cut deep gashes into the stalks. Put the whole vegetable into a covered pot containing about one to one and one-half inches of boiling salted water. Cook for about 10 minutes or until the vegetable is tender but crisp. Drain and serve with a lightly flavored delicate sauce.

CORN—When your corn is as high as an elephant's eye it's time to stop looking for elephants and start looking for darkened silk, track shoes and boiling water . . . in that order. Watch your corn carefully and when the silks show the first signs of turning dark, get on your mark. Allow the ears to remain on the stalks a little while longer, but keep watching. When the silks are dark and a bit dried out looking, get ready. Start a pot of unsalted water boiling on your range. Pick corn by snapping the ears off the stalk. When you've picked them, start running. Move as quickly as you can in the direction of your kitchen. Husk the corn immediately, and place the ears into the waiting boiling water. Cover the pot. Cook for no more than five minutes, remove with tongs, add butter or margarine, salt and pepper and ENJOY!! That's what it's all about.

A few more thoughts about corn. If you can't eat the ears immediately after picking, remove the husks and keep in a cool place. The fantastic, sugar-sweet quality starts to go soon after picking, but keeping the ears in a cool place helps a bit. Some corn-eating experts claim the corn holds its golden color better if one layer (and one layer only) of husk is left on the ear when cooking. That's Barbara's belief and since she does the cooking . . . that's how we eat our corn.

CUCUMBER—Asians have known and enjoyed this vegetable for over 4,000 years. We've come into the picture much more recently, but what a picture it is. There are so many different ways of preparing cucumbers it would take a complete book just to list them. Start picking cukes when they are about six to eight inches long and about the size of a silver dollar around. Pick them before they get any fatter and while they are dark green. Fat, yellowed cucumbers are usually not worth saving.

Always pick cucumbers late in the day when the vine's leaves are dry. Moving among wet leaves to pick these vegetables may spread disease and ruin your entire crop. Check the vines every day and cut the cucumbers carefully off the vine with garden clippers or a small knife. Be especially careful that you neither cut the vines nor step on any as you harvest your crop. Vines that are injured die and do not send out any new or replacement shoots below the injury.

If the cucumbers are lean and firm, the skin needn't be peeled away. Just trim ends, slice into any shape that pleases you, chill and serve. Slightly fatter cucumbers, with tougher skins and many, many seeds, should be peeled and the seeds scraped out and discarded.

Though most Americans prefer their cukes cold and crisp, there is something to say for their flavor when cooked. To try this for yourself, wash the cucumber in cold water and cut off both ends. Cut the cucumber in half and drop into about one inch of salted, boiling water and cook for about six minutes in a covered saucepan.

EGGPLANT—This magnificent, dark, shiny, purple treat from your garden will prove, once again, that what you buy in the supermarket can compare with home-grown vegetables in name only. The plump, firm masterpieces you see suspended from this very beautiful bush are a far cry from the sorry-looking things sold by most stores and markets.

Cut the fruit from the plant when they are about four inches in diameter. If you let an eggplant get much bigger it becomes poor tasting and full of seeds. Harvest this vegetable as close to cooking time as possible, for when they are off the vine for more than four or five days—even when kept in a cool place—they become almost as unattractive and tasteless as the store-bought kind.

With eggplant, to peel or not to peel? That is the question. The answer? If you want to peel, then peel. If you don't, then don't. All you need do to cook an eggplant is to cut or slice

These black beauties are carefully mulched to protect them against bugs, diseases and rotting. Not many like these in supermarkets.

(your choice) and follow your favorite recipe. Eggplant is unbelievably adaptable so you can sauté it, boil it, fry it and bake it. To prepare it the simplest way, just drop the cut-up eggplant into boiling, salted water, cover and cook at a boil for about six minutes.

LETTUCE—Whether you have chosen loose leaf lettuce or head lettuce, you are in for a treat the first time you bite into crunchy, crisp, delicious, home-grown garden lettuce. To harvest the leaf types, simply cut off as many leaves as you want, wash and eat. Head types should be severed from their stalks leaving about one inch of stalk above ground. If the weather is right, this little stalk stub will sprout a new growth and you will be lucky enough to start all over again with none of the work.

So few people cook lettuce that we will skip it here, and assume that most people prefer it cool, crisp and crunchy.

ONIONS—Known to man since the beginning of recorded history, onions have always been regarded as important parts of most ethnic cooking. Whether using the tops of chives or scallions or the bulbs of shallots, garlic or globe onions, the taste, smell and flavor are not soon forgotten.

To harvest this aromatic vegetable you must adapt your ways to the particular vegetable. For example, chives are harvested with a pair of scissors. That's our young son's favorite job—going out to cut as many as mommy needs for whatever she is making. He just snips off the amount needed. Scallions and shallots can be pulled from the ground and either eaten raw or cooked. For these smaller relatives, sometimes called green onions, or spring onions, the whole vegetable, bulb and top, is eaten. Garlic should be pulled from the ground, allowed to dry in the sun for a day and stored in a cool dry place. A single clove or part of a clove can be broken off and used as needed.

Globe onions, the kind you usually get when you ask for onions in the store, are pulled from the ground and allowed to dry in the sun for a day or two so a paper-like shell forms over the bulb. Cut off the top, about two inches above the bulb and store in a cool, dry place. When your recipe calls for onions, peel them under cold, running water (to try to eliminate the usual flood of tears). Use as your recipe directs, but for sheer joy, slice a fresh onion onto hamburgers, various cold meats, fish sandwiches or anything else that needs and deserves a flavor pickup.

PEAS—Another old, old favorite, peas also reach the highest excellence when grown in the home garden. Harvest your peas when the pods show bumps along their sides. Do not wait too long after the peas show in the pods or they will become too tough to be considered top quality. Remember, it is the *petits pois*, the tiny peas that are most highly prized. Do your picking early in the morning or late in the afternoon, but never during the hottest part of the day. Use as soon as possible for the sweetest taste and finest quality.

Get peas ready for the pot by pinching the pods between your thumb and forefinger and zipping out the peas. Cook peas in about an inch of salted, boiling water in a covered saucepan for six or seven minutes.

PEPPER—Red or green, makes no difference (almost) as long as they're sweet. Peppers remain green while they are growing, but as soon as they reach maturity they turn red. Though most gardeners pick and eat the peppers while they are green, some more patient gardeners, wait until they turn red to do their harvesting. Clip peppers from their bush any time they have reached the size you want. At season's end, just before frost, pull up the whole bush and hang, upside down in a cool, dry spot. The peppers left on the bush will keep well for a few weeks.

Preparation of green peppers (or sweet red) consists of washing, cutting off the stem and removing the seeds and the membrane from the center. Wash again so any seeds loosened in the process float out. If you are going to stuff your peppers, leave them whole and you are all finished with that part of your preparation. To cook slices, rings, bits and pieces, drop into salted, boiling water for about four minutes. For another taste, sauté rings, slices and pieces in butter for a few minutes and remove when tender but crisp.

POTATO—Though many say it is foolish to grow potatoes in a home garden when they are readily available in all stores, gardeners who had the space and haven't listened have been delighted with the results.

Dig potatoes when the plant's leaves start to turn brown and continue to dig until all are out of the ground and all plants are dead. Allow skins to toughen by leaving potatoes on the ground in the sun for a day or two.

Garden-grown potatoes rarely need peeling. Scrub with a vegetable brush under cold, running water and either bake white potatoes for 60 minutes and sweet potatoes for 90 minutes in a 350°F. oven; or boil in an inch and one-half of salted water for twenty to thirty minutes; or as directed in the particular recipe you are using. Check frequently using a fork to prevent overcooking. Remember to always keep the water after boiling.

While white potatoes can be stored in 50°F. temperatures for up to four or five months, sweet potatoes are much more perishable and should be used up more quickly.

PUMPKIN—If you had the room to grow these big orange beauties you'd have plenty of jack-o'-lanterns, pumpkin pies and a surprisingly pleasant vegetable. They should be cut from the vine when they are mature and definitely before the first frost. Those which cannot be used immediately can be stored in a moist area with temperature kept at about 50°F.

To cook pumpkin, cut in half and remove all strings and seeds. Peel and wash in cold water. Cut into cubes and cook in one and one-half inches of lightly salted, boiling water for about 30 minutes. Check for tenderness. Can also be baked, sautéed or pureed.

RADISHES—These are the fastest growing vegetables around. In just about three weeks radishes go from seed to table. They may be pulled when mature or even a bit before. Pull them before they become larger than a dime in diameter.

Most people simply wash and eat them with a bit of salt and pepper, or thinly sliced and placed atop a salted, buttered cracker.

RHUBARB—The most important thing to remember about rhubarb is *never, never* eat the leaves. These are definitely not "greens" and must be thrown away immediately. They contain a poison, oxalic acid, that can, if eaten give you a very bad time. Harvest the stalks lightly the second year and fully the third year and thereafter. Always pull the stalks to harvest, never cut them. Give the outer stalks a pull and a twist and you've got it.

Wash, cut and boil in a little water for about 20 minutes. Can also be stewed, baked or steamed.

SPINACH—Spinach and all of its leafy green cousins grow well in the home garden and are a delight to eye and palate. Harvested and prepared much the same as spinach are: chard, beet tops, mustard greens, collards and kale. If you are a daredevil, add dandelion, sorrel and watercress to this list.

Harvest chard and spinach (interchangeable in most recipes) by snapping off leaves at their base. Plants will continue to send out new shoots and you'll have continuous greens.

The general cooking instructions for the leafy part of these vegetables are simple and to the point. Wash, tear, cook in one-half inch salted, boiling water for three to five minutes or until tender but crisp.

SQUASH—There are two basic kinds of squash and they are grouped under the terms summer and winter squash. Aside from the time they grow and are harvested, there are some other differences between these squash types. For example, summer squash are eaten when the rind and seeds are soft and the vegetable is very, very young. Winter squash are ready for eating when the rind is hard and quite tough. Some summer squash are pattypan, crookneck, cocozelle and zucchini. Winter squash include acorn, hubbard, butternut, banana and turban.

Harvest summer squash as they become mature but before the rinds harden. Keep cutting squash to prevent them from becoming seedy and hard rinded. Use as soon as possible because summer varieties do not keep well. Winter squash is ready for harvesting when the color of the rind becomes more intense (butternut goes from soft yellow to tan) and the rind becomes hard. To remove them from the vine use a sharp knife or a pair of clippers. Don't pull them off the vine. Allow them to lie in the field for one to two weeks. The squash ripen, but do not get any larger. Get them out of the field and into 50° F. storage before the first frost.

The simplest way to prepare summer squash is to wash with a brush, but don't peel. Cut off each end, cut into slices or dice and cook in a covered pan holding one inch of boiling, salted water, for about 10 minutes. Drain, season, add butter or cheese and serve.

Winter squash should be washed, cut into portion-size pieces and cooked in one inch of boiling water in a covered pan for about 30 minutes. Better yet, cut in half, remove pits, sprinkle with sugar and cinnamon, dot with butter and bake at 400°F. for 45 minutes to one hour, until tender.

TOMATO—What more could be said about home-grown tomatoes than we have already said about the other vegetables that come from your own garden? For us, the crowning glory is always the first red, ripe tomato of the season. For us, home-grown tomatoes are both a blessing and a curse for, since we moved into our home in the country, and planted our very first garden, we have been hooked. After tasting our own tomatoes, we have never, no never (not even hardly ever) bought a tomato in a local market. So, the winter months drag slowly by without even one small fresh tomato (or cucumber either, for the same reason) to add color and excitement to our salad bowl. We keep telling ourselves that summer isn't so far away.

Be sure you pick your tomatoes every day once they start to ripen and only when the leaves are dry. Eat them raw, eat them cooked, eat them alone or with something else. We'll say no more.

HERBS—If you have never cooked with herbs this is a perfect time and the perfect opportunity to begin. It would really be a pity to have a vegetable garden and not enjoy the fun and beauty offered by growing herbs, to say nothing of the delightful flavors they add to your cooking. Here are the harvesting suggestions for some of the more popular herbs you will enjoy growing and using.

Anise - Use the fresh leaves and seeds of this plant. Clip leaves as required. To get seed, cut off the flower clusters when they have matured and allow them to dry in a cool, dry spot.

Basil - Can be used as fresh leaves or after leaves have been dried. After plants flower, cut and strip leaves and allow to dry in a cool, dark area.

Caraway - Use the seeds of this plant for a real taste treat. To get seeds, cut seed pods from plant and allow to dry. Cull seed from dried heads and store. Leaves can also be used, but very sparingly.

Chervil - Can be used either fresh or dry. Used fresh it can be chopped and used like parsley. To dry, use oven heat for a few minutes and then put dried leaves in tightly covered jars.

Chives - Use fresh as it comes from the garden. If you must, dry the leaves but don't be surprised at the relative lack of flavor. To harvest the leaves, simply cut as much as needed with a pair of scissors and use immediately.

Coriander - Seeds only are usually used from this herb. Cut the stalks when the seed heads appear ripe. Allow to dry (out of the sun) in a cool, dry spot. Take seeds out and store in a jar. If you can stand the smell, leaves can be used in some dishes.

Dill - Use the whole sprig on this one. Just cut sprigs (stalk and leaf combined) and hang, upside down in a cool spot for drying. Leaves and seeds can be used separately or together.

Fennel - Remove seeds from pods and use sparingly with vegetables and dairy dishes. Leaves, too, can be used in various dishes.

Marjoram - Can be used fresh or dried. Cut leaves and either chop up for use fresh, or dry in sun or oven and store in jars.

Mint - Both peppermint and spearmint are used just as they come from the garden or dried and stored. Cut leaves when full and dark green. Use as soon as possible or dry and store in jars.

Oregano - Really wild marjoram. Has same harvest and storage directions. Very popular on and in Italian dishes.

Parsley - Usually used fresh, but dried leaf flakes also used. Cut fresh leaves and use as garnish or flavoring. Dry in oven and store for later use.

Rosemary - Crushed fresh leaves are welcome addition to many recipes. To dry leaves, crush first, then dry and store in jars. Use sparingly and according to directions.

Sage - This herb is best when chopped very, very fine, or in the case of the dried version, powdered. Cut only the succulent tips of the plant and dry in oven before making into powder. Fresh leaves are far superior to the dried version, so use sparingly.

Savory - This herb, too, can be used both fresh and dried. Cut leaves from plant and use as they are or pull entire plant out of ground to dry. Then, strip off leaves and store in jar.

Tarragon - If you must, dry them. If you can, use the leaves fresh. A great deal of flavor is lost in drying. Fresh leaves are especially good with some of the naturally more highly flavored vegetables.

Thyme - Only the dried leaves are used from this plant, but be very careful; a little bit goes a long, long way toward making some good recipes become outstanding.

CHAPTER 4

Putting It All Together

WITH ALL THE basics behind us, it's now time for some special vegetable recipes. Some are unusual. Some are usual. All are surprisingly delicious. To find out what we mean by "surprisingly delicious" you're going to have to take a chance and try some new things (at least they will be new to you) while ridding yourself of the vegetable prejudices and hang-ups you've lived with for many years. We did—and we're glad.

When our garden was successful we tried growing different vegetables—ones we thought we didn't like. When we were successful at growing these we had to find a way to use them (how many eggplant and zucchini can you give away each year?). When we discovered a particularly tasty dish and, in our enthusiasm, repeated the recipe to all who would listen, we were often greeted with shocked surprise ... "You ... eating eggplant?" Yes, we now eat eggplant and squash and many other things we had never eaten, nor had the slightest inclination to try. We were, as are many others, in a food rut, going along eating the same few things all the time. We had no idea of the fun and the changes an organic garden and some good, simple recipes would bring to our lives and our dinner table.

There has been no attempt at gourmet cooking or gourmet-type recipes. The reason for this is simply that in our house there

51

is no gourmet cook. The philosophy of the resident cook calls for healthful, well-balanced meals that are nice looking, tasty, easy and fast.

Please note that we stress the importance of "doing your own thing." Combine vegetables, experiment with sauces, spices and seasonings you have not used before. When certain vegetables are really plentiful in your garden, take a small amount, experiment with its preparation and let the family taste. Several recipes in this chapter just "happened" that way and are now standards on our menu. Try two different recipes at one meal, for example, by cutting a vegetable like eggplant in half and preparing it either in two different ways or the same way, but with a variety of seasonings.

The basic suggestions for cooking all the vegetables you'll be likely to grow in a home garden can be found in Chapter 3. Use these as a starting point. Then, start doing your own thing according to your tastes. Make additions, corrections or deletions as you prepare the recipes. If you like more or less salt, pepper, oregano or whatever . . . go right ahead and make the adjustment. If you want to add more vegetables or take away a few, be our guest. Have a good time. Give your imagination a chance and give these home-grown foods and combinations an opportunity to delight you as they did us.

ASPARAGUS

Asparagus Casserole

12 asparagus	1 cup bread crumbs
3 eggs	1 cup diced cheddar cheese
1 teaspoon salt	1 cup milk
1/4 teaspoon pepper	3 tablespoons margarine

Cook, drain asparagus and cut into two-inch pieces. Beat eggs. Add salt, pepper, bread crumbs, diced cheese and milk. Fold in asparagus. Pour into greased casserole (1 ½ quart). Pour melted margarine over top. Bake at 350°F. for thirty minutes. Nice because it can be made earlier in the day. Simply add margarine when time to heat. *Serves 4.*

Asparagus with Crumb Topping

1/3 cup melted butter or margarine
1 minced onion

2/3 cup bread crumbs
15 spears cooked asparagus

Pour melted butter into small saucepan. Add minced onion. Sauté until translucent. Add bread crumbs. Remove from heat. Toss with *fork* until crumbs, onions and butter are mixed. Put into small serving dish. Let each person spoon mixture over asparagus. *Serves 4-5.*

Asparagus Roll-ups

Very thin slices of American
   cheese

Cooked asparagus spears
Buttered bread crumbs

Allow cheese to soften at room temperature. Carefully and gently roll one asparagus in one slice of cheese. Arrange on ovenproof platter. Sprinkle buttered bread crumbs on top. Place in 200°F. oven only about five minutes. Serve with pie server or, even better, wide pancake turner. Fine as a vegetable side dish for meat dinner or as a luncheon dish with a salad and fresh hot rolls or home-baked herb bread. *Figure 3 spears per person.*

Asparagus Romano

Cooked asparagus
Romano cheese

Finely diced tomatoes
Parmesan cheese

Lay asparagus on ovenproof platter. Place thin slices of Romano cheese over asparagus. Sprinkle diced tomatoes over top. Sprinkle Parmesan cheese over top. Bake at 350°F. about twenty minutes until cheese melts and browns.

BEANS

Creamy Green Beans

2 cups fresh green beans
1/4 cup fresh diced chives

1/2 cup plain yogurt (or sour
   cream)

Cook green beans. Drain. Add chives. Add yogurt. Stir gently. *Serves 4.*

Green Bean Salad

1 pound green beans

4 hard-cooked eggs

2 onions

Mayonnaise

Salt and pepper to taste

Cook green beans until just tender. Chop very, very fine or put through grinder. Put eggs through grinder or chop very fine. Do the same with the onions. Mix well. Add enough mayonnaise to hold mixture together. Add salt and pepper to taste. Refrigerate for several hours before serving. May be served on lettuce leaves, on a sandwich, or stuffed into a hollowed-out tomato or pepper. *Serves 4.*

Crunchy Green Bean Casserole

1 tablespoon butter

1 cup diced onions

2 cups crisp cooked green
   beans

1 can condensed golden mush-
   room soup

Melt butter in small skillet. Sauté diced onions until dark and crispy. Place on paper toweling to drain. Stir together beans and soup (do not add water to soup, use just as it comes from can). Sprinkle crispy onions over top. Place in oven at 300°F. about ten to fifteen minutes to heat through. Serve at once. *Serves 4-5.*

Beans and Tomatoes

1 pound cooked fresh green
   beans

2 large tomatoes

Salt

Oregano

Italian dressing

Cut beans into one-inch pieces. Dice tomatoes. Season with salt and oregano. Toss. Pour Italian dressing over top. Toss and serve. *Serves 4-5.*

LIMA BEANS

Lima Bean Succotash

1 cup cooked lima beans
1 cup cooked corn
1/2 cup cooked peas

2 tablespoons butter or margarine
3/4 teaspoon salt
1/8 teaspoon pepper

Heat in double boiler until hot enough to serve. *Serves 4-5.*

Lima Bean Casserole

8 frankfurters or sausages
2 cups cooked lima beans
1 cup chopped tomatoes

1/2 cup chopped green pep-
per (optional)
Salt
Pepper

Slice frankfurters or sausages in one-inch pieces. Mix all ingredients. Season to taste. Place in casserole. Bake at 350°F. about twenty-five minutes (just until warmed through). *Serves 4 (for dinner).*

Grandma's Lima Beans

Chicken giblets
1 teaspoon salt
3 cups cold water

2 cups fresh lima beans
3-4 tablespoons brown sugar

Place chicken giblets and salt in water in large saucepan. Simmer until giblets are soft, about one hour. Add beans and brown sugar. Stir until sugar dissolves. Continue cooking until lima beans are tender (but not soft), about twenty to twenty-five minutes. Most of the water will boil off and you will be left with a slightly thickened brown sauce. Keep an eye on the beans to be sure that too much water doesn't boil out or they will burn. This is an excellent side dish for roast chicken for obvious reasons. The sauce should be thick when served and not at all runny.
Serves 4-5.

Baked Lima Beans

2 cups cooked lima beans
1 onion (diced)
1/4 cup brown sugar

1/2 cup sour cream (or yogurt)
Salt
Pepper

Mix all ingredients. Place in casserole. Bake at 350°F. for twenty-five minutes. *Serves 5* (very rich and filling).

BEETS

Borscht

2 cups shredded fresh beets
1 large grated onion
2 teaspoons salt

3 tablespoons sugar
1/4 cup lemon juice

Mix beets, onion and salt. Cover and cook over low heat for about one to one and one-quarter hours. Stir in sugar until dissolved. Slowly add lemon juice and stir until thoroughly mixed. Taste and adjust seasoning if desired. Chill for several hours before serving. This is a favorite summer lunch. Serve in a tall glass, with a heaping tablespoon of sour cream stirred in. Also delicious served in a soup bowl, with a hot boiled potato, with or without sour cream. *Serves 4 (as a soup).*

Harvard Beets

1/3 cup sugar
1 tablespoon cornstarch
1/4 teaspoon salt

1/3 cup vinegar
2 cups cooked, diced beets
2 tablespoons butter

Mix and heat sugar, cornstarch, salt, vinegar over double boiler. Continue mixing until liquid becomes clear. Add beets and warm through. When ready to serve, add butter. Remove from heat and stir until butter melts. Serve immediately. *Serves 4-5.*

Beet Relish

2 cups beets	2 tablespoons sugar
2 cups cabbage	1 1/2 teaspoons salt
2 tablespoons diced onion	Vinegar

Cook and dice beets. Wash and finely dice cabbage. Mix beets, cabbage and onion in large bowl. Add sugar and salt. Add about 1/2 cup vinegar. Taste. Adjust if necessary. Toss gently. Tastes better if allowed to stand at least twenty-four hours before using. *Serves 8.*

Pickled Beets

2 cups thinly sliced cooked beets	1 cup water
2 medium onions sliced very thin	1/2 cup vinegar
	1/4 cup sugar
Salt	

Mix and gently shake beets and onions. Salt and shake again. Mix water, vinegar and sugar. Stir to dissolve sugar. Pour over beets and allow to marinate several hours before serving. *Serves 6-8.*

BROCCOLI

Broccoli Onion Casserole

3 cups cooked broccoli	1 teaspoon salt
2 cups tiny onions (cooked and drained)	1/4 teaspoon pepper
2 cups milk (or light cream)	1/3 - 1/4 cup flour
1/2 cup butter	2 slices American cheese

Combine broccoli and onions in a casserole. Combine milk, butter, salt and pepper over double boiler. Stir until warm. Add flour slowly until sauce thickens. Pour over casserole. Cut cheese slices in half to form four triangles. Arrange on top of casserole. Bake at 350°F. about twenty to thirty minutes. Nice also because everything can be prepared ahead, then cheese added and put into oven when ready to serve. *Serves 6-7.*

Sautéed Broccoli

1/4 cup butter (or margarine)	1 clove garlic
2 medium onions, minced	2 cups broccoli
1 red pepper	1 teaspoon salt

Melt butter in skillet. Add onion, pepper and garlic (cut clove in three or four pieces). Simmer about ten minutes. Wash and chop broccoli into bite-size pieces. Remove garlic. Add broccoli and salt. Stir gently. Cover and simmer about fifteen minutes. Serve immediately. *Serves 4-5.*

Italian Style Broccoli

3 tablespoons olive oil	1 teaspoon salt
1 clove garlic	1/8 teaspoon pepper
2 cups broccoli	1 teaspoon oregano
1 cup chopped tomatoes	

Heat olive oil in skillet. Add garlic, cook until brown, then discard. Add washed and chopped broccoli (no smaller than bite-size pieces), tomatoes, salt and pepper. Cook for about fifteen minutes. Add oregano. Cook in covered pan five minutes more. Serve immediately. *Serves 5-6.*

Broccoli Loaf

2 tablespoons butter or margarine	2 cups dry bread crumbs
1 medium onion, minced	2 eggs, beaten
3 cups cooked chopped broccoli	1 teaspoon salt
	1/4 teaspoon pepper

Melt butter in small skillet. Sauté onion. Add onion (with butter) to broccoli. Add rest of ingredients. Pour into greased loaf pan. Bake at 350°F. for thirty minutes. Turn out on serving dish. Serve with cream sauce poured over top at last minute or with crumbled hard-cooked egg sprinkled over top. *Serves 6-8.*

BRUSSELS SPROUTS

Sautéed Brussels Sprouts

4 tablespoons butter or margarine
1 medium onion
3 cups Brussels sprouts
1/2 cup chicken stock or broth

1 teaspoon salt
1/4 teaspoon pepper
1 tablespoon chopped parsley
2 teaspoons chopped chives

Melt butter. Slice onion *very* thin and separate into rings. Sauté gently in butter. Prepare sprouts for cooking. Add sprouts and remainder of ingredients except parsley and chives. Simmer gently in covered pan for ten to twelve minutes, until sprouts are tender but crisp. Serve at once with parsley and chives sprinkled over top. *Serves 6-8.*

Brussels Sprouts with Garlic and Cheese

3 cups Brussels sprouts
5 tablespoons olive oil
2 cloves garlic
1 onion, minced

1 teaspoon salt
1/4 teaspoon pepper
1/2 cup grated Parmesan cheese

Wash sprouts and prepare for cooking. Heat olive oil in baking pan or casserole. Put in garlic and onion. Let simmer for about five to seven minutes. Add Brussels sprouts, salt and pepper. Stir thoroughly and simmer five minutes more. Sprinkle Parmesan cheese over top and place in oven. Bake ten minutes at 325°F. *Serves 6-8.*

Brussels Sprouts with Chestnuts

3 tablespoons butter or margarine
2 cups cooked Brussels sprouts

1 cup sliced cooked chestnuts
1 teaspoon salt
1/4 teaspoon pepper

Melt butter. Toss all ingredients together. Pour melted butter over top and serve. *Serves 5.*

Brussels Sprouts Pie

4 cups cooked mashed po- tatoes	1/4 cup milk
	2 tablespoons butter
1 teaspoon salt	2-3 cups Brussels sprouts
1/4 teaspoon pepper	Cheese (optional)

Whip mashed potatoes with salt, pepper, milk and butter. Spoon into pie pan and press into shape of pan. Carefully arrange the individual sprouts to fill the potato pie shell. You may (if you wish) cut pie-slice-shaped pieces of American cheese and arrange over top. Parmesan or grated cheddar cheese may also be sprinkled over top of pie. Heat at 350°F. until warmed through. Cut and serve as you would a pie, using a pie knife. Both attractive and tasty. *Serves 6-8.*

CABBAGE

Cole Slaw

1 small head cabbage (red or green)	Salt
	1 1/2 cups water
1 carrot	1 1/4 cups vinegar
1 green pepper	1/2 cup sugar
1 small onion	4 tablespoons mayonnaise

Shred cabbage, wash and put into large bowl. Dice carrot, pepper and onion. Add to cabbage. Salt to taste and mix well Combine water, vinegar, sugar and mayonnaise. Pour over cabbage mixture. Mix thoroughly and refrigerate in covered bowl. Mix several times during day allowing cabbage to marinate well. This is best prepared in the morning to be served for dinner. *Serves 6.*

Cole Slaw — Serving Suggestions

1. Wash and core but do not peel an apple. Cut into twelfths and add to cole slaw.
2. Add 1/2 cup cooked diced red beets for color and an interesting flavor.

3. Instead of marinade above, mix 1 cup yogurt, vinegar, sugar, salt and pepper. Taste, adjust flavoring. Pour over cabbage. Marinate several hours.

(Un) Stuffed Cabbage

1 large head of cabbage	2 pieces sour salt
1/2 cup tomato juice	2 pounds ground beef
1 diced onion	1 teaspoon salt
1 teaspoon salt	1/8 teaspoon pepper
1 teaspoon paprika	1 grated carrot
Juice of 1 whole lemon (or	1 minced or grated onion
1 teaspoon lemon juice)	1 egg
1/2 cup sugar	

Cut cabbage into quarters. Remove core. Shred about one-half- to three-quarters inch thick. Into the bottom of the pot put: tomato juice, onion, salt, paprika, lemon juice, sugar and sour salt. Stir to mix. Put about one-third of cabbage into bottom of pot. To the ground beef add: salt, pepper, carrot, onion, and egg. Shape about one half of the meat mixture into meatballs (6 or 7). Arrange them on top of cabbage. Cover with one-third of cabbage. Make rest of meat into meatballs and place on top of cabbage. Put in last third of cabbage. If cooking in regular pot (6-quart Dutch oven) cover cabbage with water—cover pot and simmer one and one-half hours. If using pressure cooker (6 quart) do not add any more liquid. Cover pot and cook for twenty-seven minutes once pressure goes up. *Serves 5-6.*

Cabbage and Tomato Casserole

1 head cabbage, shredded	1/4 teaspoon pepper
2 medium tomatoes, sliced	1 cup bread crumbs
1 teaspoon salt	1/2 cup Parmesan cheese

Butter a baking dish or casserole. Arrange in layers, first cabbage, then tomatoes, seasoning, bread crubs and cheese. Continue until all ingredients are used up. Bake at 350°F. for thirty minutes until top cheese melts and browns. *Serves 5.*

Cabbage and Vegetable Skillet

2 tablespoons butter or margarine	1/2 cup chopped chives
1 medium head cabbage, shredded	1 cup diced tomatoes (or 1 cup thick tomato sauce)
3 stalks finely diced celery	1 teaspoon salt
1 green pepper, thinly sliced	1/4 teaspoon pepper

Melt butter in large heavy skillet. Add all other ingredients. Mix well. Cover and simmer eight to ten minutes until all ingredients are tender but crisp. Do not uncover while cooking. *Serves 5.*

CARROTS

Carrots and Squash

2 tablespoons minced onion	2 cups summer squash
2 tablespoons margarine or butter	1 teaspoon salt
2 cups baby carrots	1/8 teaspoon pepper

Sauté onion in butter for about ten minutes. Add carrots and squash. Season. Add a little water if necessary. Add salt and pepper. Cover and simmer gently until vegetables are tender but still crisp (about twelve to eighteen minutes). *Serves 4.*

Carrot Tzimmes

3 pounds meat for stew (beef)	4 large sweet potatoes
2 cups boiling water	10 small carrots
1 pound pitted prunes	1/4 cup brown sugar (packed)
1 teaspoon salt	2 tablespoons honey
1/4 teaspoon pepper	2 tablespoons lemon juice

Brown meat, add water. Add prunes and cook in covered saucepan for one and one-half hours. Add all other ingredients.

Cover and cook one more hour, until everything is tender. If you prefer the easy way—simply combine all ingredients (use 1/2 cup water instead of 2 cups) and cook for twenty minutes in pressure cooker. *Serves 6.*

Carrots à l'Orange

8-10 carrots	1/2 cup orange juice
3 tablespoons butter or margarine	2 oranges, peeled and sliced
	1/8 teaspoon nutmeg
1/4 cup brown sugar	

Wash carrots and scrub with stiff brush. Cut in half the long way. Cook in small amount of boiling salted water until tender but still crisp. Meanwhile, melt butter (or margarine) in heavy skillet. Add sugar and orange juice. Let bubble two to three minutes. Add carrots; turn frequently to glaze well, over medium heat. Top with orange slices and sprinkle nutmeg over top. Serve at once. *Serves 6.*

CAULIFLOWER

Cauliflower Salad

1 large head cauliflower	1 green pepper
1 or 2 tomatoes	1 cucumber

Cook cauliflower till crisp—do not overcook. Drain and chill. Wash and dice tomatoes and pepper. Wash, peel and dice cucumber. Mix and toss gently. Pour on favorite dressing, toss. Sprinkle with fresh parsley. *Serves 6-8.*

Cauliflower and Mushroom Casserole

3 cups cooked cauliflower	1 can French fried onions
1 can condensed cream of mushroom soup	

Mix cauliflower with undiluted soup. Stir and pour into casserole. Sprinkle French fried onions over top. Heat until warmed through. *Serves 6-8.*

Special Cauliflower

1 cauliflower	2 tablespoons parsley
1/2 cup heavy cream	

Cook cauliflower until tender but crisp. Warm cream just a bit. Stir cream gently into cauliflower. Sprinkle with fresh chopped parsley. Serve immediately. *Serves 4.*

Cauliflower Marinade

1 cauliflower	1/2 teaspoon salt
1/4 cup olive oil	1/4 teaspoon pepper
1/4 cup salad oil	1/4 teaspoon dry mustard
2 tablespoons wine vinegar	2 cloves garlic (minced)

Cook cauliflower—break into flowerets. Bring to boil. Boil eight to ten minutes. Mix remainder of ingredients. Drain cauliflower. Pour marinade over cauliflower and allow to stand overnight. Same marinade may also be used over fresh sliced tomatoes or cooked green beans. *Serves 4-5.*

CORN

Roasted Corn

Husk corn and remove all silk and damaged portions. Brush with melted butter seasoned with salt and pepper. Wrap tightly in aluminum foil and roast thirty minutes at 400°F.

Ruffitz's Corn "Critters"

1 cup corn (or creamed corn)	1 small minced onion
1 egg	1 teaspoon salt
1/3 cup milk	1 teaspoon baking powder
1 tablespoon melted butter	About 7 tablespoons flour

To corn, add egg, milk, melted butter and minced onion. Stir in salt and baking powder. Add flour a little at a time to make good batter (not too thin or it will run and not hold its shape). Melt about 2 tablespoons butter (or oil) on griddle. Drop by large spoonfuls onto griddle. Brown, turn, brown other side, drain and serve. These are, of course, corn fritters, but the first time we made them our daughter didn't know what a fritter was and called them "corn critters." Naturally that's what we all call them now. *Makes about one dozen.*

Corn Pudding

1 green pepper, diced	Salt
1 onion, minced	Pepper
3 tablespoons butter	2 tablespoons sugar
2 eggs	1 cup milk
2 cups cooked corn	

Sauté pepper and onion in butter about ten minutes until tender but still crisp. Separate eggs (if you want to go to the bother; sometimes we don't). Mix all ingredients but egg whites. Whip egg whites until stiff then fold into corn mixture. Bake in shallow casserole about thirty minutes at 350°F. Nutmeg may be sprinkled over top when ready to serve. *Serves 4-5.*

Tossed Chicken Salad

1 1/2 cups leftover cooked diced chicken	1 cup uncooked fresh baby peas
1 cup cooked corn	1 cucumber
2 tomatoes, diced	1/2 head lettuce, in bite-size pieces

Mix and toss. Pour on French dressing. Serve chilled. *Serves 3-4.*

Spicy Vegetable Salad

1 cup diced Italian sausage	1/2 cup cooked squash
1/2 cup cooked corn	1/2 cup diced green or red pepper
1/2 cup snap beans	

Mix and toss. Season with salt and pepper. Mix equal parts of oil and vinegar. Pour over top. Sprinkle one tablespoon fresh parsley over top. *Serves 6-8.*

Corn, Zucchini and Tomato Casserole

1 cup corn	1 teaspoon salt
1 cup diced zucchini	1/8 teaspoon pepper
1 cup diced fresh tomatoes	1 teaspoon sugar
1/2 cup diced green pepper	2 tablespoons butter
1/2 cup diced onion	3/4 cup bread crumbs

Melt butter in large skillet. Sauté all other ingredients (not bread crumbs) about ten to fifteen minutes until tender but still crisp. Pour into shallow greased casserole. Sprinkle bread crumbs over top. Bake about ten to fifteen minutes at 350°F. until top starts to turn light golden brown. A slice of American cheese can be cut into four triangular pieces and arranged atop the bread crumbs and allowed to start to melt into the casserole before serving. *Serves 6-8.*

CUCUMBERS
Sweet-and-Sour Cucumber Slices

5 long, thin cucumbers	1 1/4 cups vinegar
(about 8 inches long, 1 1/2	1 1/2 cups water
inches in diameter)	1/2 cup sugar
Salt	1 onion (optional)

Wash and peel cucumbers. If preferred, wash but do not peel. Slice very thin. Place in large bowl. Salt heavily. Mix thoroughly using hands. Let stand one hour. Drain any liquid. Combine vinegar, water and sugar. Mix until sugar is dissolved. Pack cucumbers into jars or bowl with cover. Add sliced onion if desired. Cover completely with vinegar mixture. Refrigerate. *Yield: 3 quart jars.*

Stuffed Cucumber

Wash and peel extra-large cucumbers. Cut in half the long way. Using a "regular" teaspoon (one that you would set on the table) run the spoon down the length of the cuke. Remove and discard all seeds and soft pulp. Fill trench and pack well with filling of your choice: chopped liver, egg salad, tuna salad, etc. Serve on bed of lettuce with tomatoes, green pepper, celery and carrot sticks. Allow one half large cucumber per person. May also be sliced and served as hors d'oeuvres. When using this way, do not mound filling above level of cucumber. Place thin slice of stuffed cucumber on slice of party rye or on round salted cracker.

Cucumber Dressing

2 large cucumbers (about 8   1/4 teaspoon salt
  inches long)   1/4 teaspoon pepper
1 very small onion   1/4 cup vinegar

Wash and peel cucumbers. Soak cukes in cold water for one hour. Drain. Cut into thick pieces and put into blender. Blend (on high) until smooth and liquid. Add remaining ingredients. Blend until smooth and liquid. Pour into one-quart jar and refrigerate.

Aunt Celia's Bread-and-Butter Pickles

2 cucumbers (about 6 inches   2 cups vinegar
  long)   1 1/2 cups sugar
5 medium onions   1/2 teaspoon turmeric
1/4 cup salt (coarse)   1 1/2 teaspoons mustard seed
2 cups water   1 teaspoon celery seed

Wash cucumbers, cut in 1/2-inch slices without paring. Peel onions and cut in 1/4-inch slices. Place layers of sliced vegetables alternately in bowl with salt. Let stand three hours. Drain and rinse well with cold water. Mix water, vinegar, sugar, turmeric, mustard and celery seed in large kettle and bring to boil. Stir until sugar is dissolved. Add cucumbers and onions and heat *thoroughly* but do not boil. Pour into hot, sterilized jars and seal immediately. *Makes 5-6 pints.*

Cucumber Hors d'Oeuvres

Toast   1/3 cup grated Parmesan
Sliced cucumber   cheese
Sliced onion   Salt
2/3 cup mayonnaise   Oregano

Using cookie cutter, shape toast, cucumber and onion. Mix mayonnaise, cheese and salt. Layer: toast, cuke and onion pouring one spoonful of mixture on each. Sprinkle on oregano. Toast under broiler two to three minutes until cheese melts and browns in 200°F. oven.

EGGPLANT
French Fried Eggplant

1 medium eggplant	2 tablespoons water or milk
1 cup cracker crumbs	Salt
1 egg	Pepper

Peel and slice eggplant. Dip into cracker crumbs. Mix together egg, two tablespoons water (or milk), salt and pepper. Dip into egg mixture then back into cracker crumbs. This makes an extra thick crust. Fry in hot vegetable oil until golden brown. Drain on paper toweling. *Serves 6.*

Monteiro's Eggplant Spread

6 tablespoons margarine	2 tablespoons vinegar
1 eggplant, peeled and diced	1 1/2 teaspoons salt
1 onion, chopped	1 teaspoon sugar
1/4 cup tomato paste	Pepper
1/4 cup sour cream (or yo- gurt)	

Melt margarine in saucepan. Add eggplant and onion to margarine. Cook until tender. Remove from heat. Add rest of ingredients. Mix well. Chill. Spread on very thin rye bread. Joan says, "Weird but delicious."

Eggplant Pancakes

1 medium eggplant	1 egg
1 onion	2 tablespoons flour
1 teaspoon salt	Vegetable oil
1/8 teaspoon pepper	

Peel and grind (or grate) eggplant. Drain liquid. Add grated onion, salt, pepper, egg and flour. Mix thoroughly. Fry in hot vegetable oil until golden brown and crisp. Drain on paper toweling. Delightful lower-calorie substitute for potato pancakes. *Makes about fifteen pancakes.*

Eggplant Parmigiana

1 large eggplant	1/2 pound mozzarella cheese
2 eggs	2 cups tomato sauce
1 teaspoon salt	1/4 - 1/2 cup grated Parme-
1/4 teaspoon pepper	san cheese

Peel eggplant, slice thin (about one-quarter inch). Beat eggs gently and add salt and pepper. Dip eggplant in eggs and fry in vegetable oil until golden brown. Drain on paper toweling. Using a two-quart casserole place a layer of eggplant, a layer of thinly sliced mozzarella cheese and a layer of tomato sauce. Repeat until all ingredients are used up. Sprinkle Parmesan cheese over top. Bake at 350°F. until done, about one-half hour. Any Parmesan cheese which is left may be added when served. *Serves 6.*

Stuffed Eggplant

Making a zig-zag design, cut off the top of a medium eggplant. Scoop out pulp (leaving about one-half inch in shell). Cook pulp until tender. Drain and mash. Mix with leftover diced chicken, or diced ham, or meat loaf. Stuff into eggplant. Cover with top of eggplant and bake about twenty minutes until filling warms through.

What a beautiful dish to put on the table. Serve one to each person. (You can even fill each one with a different leftover. Sometimes we get very efficient and freeze one leftover portion of meat. This is a fantastic way to utilize leftovers. Defrost, dice, mix with rice or vegetable or eggplant, stuff eggplant with mixture and bake.)

ONION

French Fried Onion Rings

Large mild onions	Salt
Milk	Pepper
Flour	

Clean and slice onions about one-quarter inch thick. Separate into rings. Lay rings into shallow dish. Pour in enough milk so rings are covered. Soak about forty minutes. Mix flour with salt and pepper. Coat onion rings with flour mixture. Fry in hot vegetable oil until golden brown. Drain on paper toweling and serve.

Creamed Onions

1 orange, peeled	1 1/4 cups milk
2 pounds tiny whole cooked onions (in cooking liquid)	2 tablespoons finely grated orange peel (optional)
2 tablespoons flour	1 teaspoon Worcestershire sauce
2 tablespoons melted butter or margarine	1/4 teaspoon dry mustard
1 teaspoon salt	Paprika

Cut orange into bite-size pieces. Simmer onions until heated (in cooking liquid); drain. In small saucepan, stir flour into melted butter to form a smooth paste. Add salt. Gradually add milk, stirring until mixture is smooth. Bring to a boil over medium heat. Stir constantly while boiling for three minutes. Stir in grated peel, Worcestershire and mustard. Pour hot sauce over drained onions; gently stir in orange pieces. Sprinkle with paprika; serve at once. *Serves 6.*

Onion/Rice Casserole

2 cups diced onions	2 cups cooked rice
4 tablespoons butter	1 teaspoon salt

Sauté onions in heavy skillet in vegetable oil until golden brown and getting a bit crispy. Remove to paper toweling and drain. Using butter or margarine, grease casserole very well. In another bowl, mix rice, onions and salt. Pour into casserole. Dot top with butter or margarine.

Bake in oven at 350°F. for twenty to twenty-five minutes until heated through and slightly golden on top. *Serves 8.*

PEAS

Puree of Peas

2 cups cooked peas	Salt
2 tablespoons light cream	Pepper
2 tablespoons butter or margarine	2 tablespoons chopped fresh chives

Put peas through sieve. Place in top of double boiler with gently boiling water below. Stir in ingredients. Stir and allow to warm through. Serve individual portions on crisp lettuce leaf. A small dollop of sour cream with crisp bacon crumbled on top may be added, if desired. *Serves 4.*

French Peas

2 cups fresh peas	Salt
1 cup tiny fresh onions	Pepper
3 tablespoons butter	

Place all ingredients in saucepan. Add one-half-inch water. Cover and cook over low heat ten to fifteen minutes, until tender; do not overcook. *Serves 4-5.*

Peas and Rice

2 cups cooked peas	Salt
2 cups cooked rice	Pepper
4 tablespoons butter or margarine	2 tablespoons chopped chives

Mix all ingredients. Put into greased casserole. Bake at 250°F. just long enough for ingredients to heat through. Great way to use up leftover rice. Wild rice may be used also. *Serves 8.*

Pea Salad

2 cups cooked cold baby peas
2 cups diced cooked chicken
1 cup diced celery

1 cup drained canned pineapple tidbits

Mix and toss all ingredients. Serve on individual beds of lettuce. *Serves 6-8.*

PEPPERS

Green Pepper/Cottage Cheese Slices

2 medium green peppers
1 medium red pepper

1 1/2 cups cottage cheese

Wash and remove tops, seeds and fibers of peppers. Trim around stems and dice into small pieces. Set aside. Mash cottage cheese and stir in green and red pepper bits. Spoon cottage cheese into peppers. Pack down firmly. Refrigerate overnight. Cut in one-half-inch slices. Red and green bits of pepper against white cheese are very attractive. Serve on bed of lettuce with tomato wedges and cucumber slices. *Serves 3-4.*

Stuffed Peppers and Tomatoes

3 large beautiful green peppers
1 more green pepper
6 hard-cooked eggs

Mayonnaise
3 large perfect tomatoes
1 seven-ounce can of tuna

Wash three peppers. Carefully cut away tops. Remove seeds. Clean, slice and dice fourth pepper. Chop eggs. Add mayonnaise to taste. Stir in diced pepper. Set aside. Wash tomatoes. Carefully cut away tops. Scoop out insides, chop and set aside. Drain and flake tuna. Add mayonnaise to taste. Stir in chopped tomato. Carefully spoon tuna mixture into three peppers, and egg mixture into tomatoes. Arrange on lettuce leaves on attractive serving dish. Lovely luncheon dish. *Serves 6.*

Pepper and Eggs

Margarine (or butter)	Pepper
1/2 green pepper	2 eggs
Salt	

Melt margarine. Clean and dice pepper. Sauté in margarine in small frying pan, about eight to ten minutes, until soft but still crisp. Scramble eggs adding salt and pepper to taste. Shake pan to spread peppers around nicely. Pour eggs into pan. Lower flame and cover. Eggs will set within a very few minutes. When set, shake pan to loosen pancake-like eggs. Slide out onto plate. Starting at one side, roll pancake up, leave it on one half of plate and put two or three slices of fresh, red, ripe tomato on the other. Or just leave the perfect pancake covering the entire plate and use another plate for rolls, toast or tomatoes. Sprinkling a pinch of oregano into the egg mixture produces a very delicious variation. *Serves 1 for lunch or 2 for breakfast.*

Guess What Peppers

Wash and remove tops, seeds and fibers of as many green peppers as you need. Blanch in boiling water for five minutes. While they are blanching stir together those warmed ingredients which you will use as a filling. Your own imagination, taste preferences, foods on hand and course to be served helps in your choice of filling. For a main meat course, quickly sauté and season ground beef and diced onion. Leftover diced beef, ham, chicken or lamb may also be combined with onion and warmed through. For a vegetable dish, use hot mashed potatoes, peas and carrots, diced sautéed green pepper and corn, zucchini, squash, eggplant. What you have is what you use. Rice is also good and this is a good way to use up leftover cooked rice. Occasionally you might use this as a silly but effective way to use up assorted one-serving leftover vegetables. Use a different stuffing in each pepper (use as many as there are members in the family). Put the top back on each pepper so no one knows what's inside. Whichever pepper you pick, you eat. Better have a fantastic dessert that night to make up for any possible "I hate thats."

POTATOES
Potato Salad

2 pounds potatoes	1 green pepper, diced
1 cup vinegar	1/2 cup diced celery
1 heaping tablespoon may-	1 small onion, minced (op-
onnaise	tional)
1/4 cup French dressing	Salt
1 carrot, diced	

Peel and cook potatoes until done but *not* soft. Cut into pieces and allow to cook while you prepare dressing. Mix together vinegar, mayonnaise, French dressing. To this add carrot, pepper, celery and onion (if desired). When potatoes are cool, salt and toss gently. Pour dressing over potatoes and mix gently. Prepare several hours before using to allow all flavors to mix and blend. *Makes about one quart.*

Potato Latkes

4 large white potatoes	1/8 teaspoon pepper
1 onion (optional)	2 tablespoons flour or matzo
2 eggs	meal
1 teaspoon salt	Vegetable oil

Peel and grate potatoes and onion. Add remainder of ingredients. Heat vegetable oil in large frying pan. Drop potato mixture into oil by using large soup spoon. Make sure fat is *very* hot or pancakes will stick. Fry until crisp and golden brown. Turn and fry on other side until crisp and brown. Remove with slotted pancake turner and drain thoroughly on paper toweling. Keep the pancakes thin. They cook more quickly and get crisper. We like ours with cold, homemade applesauce. *Serves 5-6.*

Variation: The potato mix may also be turned into a *very* well-greased 8-inch shallow round baking pan and baked at 350°F. for one hour or until top crust is crisp and darker than golden brown. This is sometimes hard to get out whole, so cut into pie-shaped wedges right at the table. (Don't use a teflon pan—cutting can ruin the surface.) This, by the way, is called Potato Kugel.

Potato Croquettes

Leftover mashed potatoes   Pepper

1 egg   Dash onion power (optional)

Salt

If you can plan ahead, make extra mashed potatoes the night before and set them aside. Mix all ingredients together. Melt margarine, butter or oil in skillet. Shape potato mixture into small patties. Fry in oil until brown. Turn and fry on other side. Drain on paper toweling. Serve immediately. They may also be placed on a cookie sheet and baked in the oven. A method that takes longer and is a bit more of a fuss involves dipping the patty in beaten egg, rolling in cracker crumbs and then frying. Also delicious.

Baked and Stuffed Potatoes

Scrub potato skin with vegetable brush. Bake at 350°F. for one hour. Cut in half and scoop out insides. May be served many ways.

1) Mix potato insides with salt and pepper. Add one tablespoon butter per potato. Mix. Spoon back into skin. Sprinkle top with onion powder and paprika. Put into oven for ten to fifteen minutes before serving.

2) Fill with mixed cooked vegetables into which you may dice potato insides. Sprinkle top with bread crumbs or Parmesan cheese. Heat in oven ten to fifteen minutes before serving.

3) Fill with hash.

4) Fill with fried chopped bacon mixed with potato.

5) Use your own imagination.

Leftover Potatoes

If baked, grate. Heat about two tablespoons vegetable oil in small skillet. Lay potatoes in so they are as flat as possible. Cover and fry until brown. Turn like pancake. Brown.

If mashed, mix with egg, salt and pepper. Shape into patties. Dip into flour, cracker crumbs or matzo meal. Melt margarine in skillet. Brown patties, turn, then drain on paper toweling.

PUMPKIN
Pumpkin Pie

2 nine-inch pie crusts	1 teaspoon cinnamon
2 eggs (stirred but not beaten)	1/2 teaspoon ginger
1 pound cooked pumpkin	1/4 teaspoon nutmeg
3/4 cup sugar	1 2/3 cups evaporated milk
Very generous pinch salt	

Mix all ingredients together in order given. Pour into pie shell. Preheat oven to 450°F. Cover pie with top shell. Seal and prick. Bake at 450°F. for fifteen minutes. Reduce oven heat to 350°F. and continue baking about twenty-five minutes (or until set, when knife inserted in center comes out clean).

Pumpkin Custard

2/3 cup pumpkin	1 egg
1 cup evaporated milk	1/8 teaspoon nutmeg
2 tablespoons sugar	1/8 teaspoon ginger

Put all ingredients in blender (or in large bowl and use beater). Briefly mix in blender. Divide mixture into five or six buttered custard cups. Set in large enough roasting pan to accommodate all cups. Put about one inch of water in pan, and place cups in pan. Bake at 325°F. for about twenty minutes, until custards are a nice golden brown and set. Serve warm (but not hot). If you can plan well enough, take them *out* of the oven when you sit down for lunch or supper—then they'll have cooled just enough for dessert. *Serves 5-6.*

Mrs. Andrews' Pumpkin Chiffon Pie

Graham cracker crust (below)	1/2 teaspoon ginger
3 beaten egg yolks	1/2 teaspoon nutmeg
3/4 cup brown sugar	1 package unflavored gelatin
1 1/2 cups cooked pumpkin	1/4 cup cold water
1/2 cup milk	3 egg whites, stiffly beaten
1/2 teaspoon salt	1/4 cup sugar
1 teaspoon cinnamon	

Combine egg yolks, brown sugar, pumpkin, milk, salt and spices. Cook in double boiler until thick, stirring constantly. Soften gelatin in cold water; stir into hot mixture. Chill until partially set. Beat egg whites; gradually add sugar, beat until stiff. Fold into gelatin mixture. Pour into graham cracker pie shell and chill several hours to set.

Graham Cracker Crust

1 1/2 cups graham cracker crumbs	1/3 cup sugar
	1/2 cup melted butter

Combine all ingredients. Press into pie pan and chill forty-five minutes.

RHUBARB

Hittleman's Rhubarb and Strawberries

5 cups sliced strawberries	10 cups rhubarb
1/4 cup sugar	1 cup water
2 tablespoons lemon juice	2 cups sugar

Sprinkle strawberries with sugar and lemon juice. Let stand to form own juices. Wash rhubarb. Cut into one-half-inch pieces. Add water and sugar. Pour into large pot. Cover. Bring to a boil. Lower heat to medium and cook at a slow boil twenty to thirty minutes, until soft. Lower heat and add strawberries. Cover and cook ten minutes more. *Yield: 5-6 quarts.*

Rhubarb Sauce

1 pound fresh rhubarb	4 tablespoons red wine
1/3 cup water	1/2 cup sugar

Cut rhubarb into one-inch pieces. Combine all ingredients. Simmer over double boiler about ten minutes. Buy individual sponge tarts (or serve individual slices of sponge or pound cake). Serve scoop of strawberry ice cream and pour sauce over top. Makes about one pint depending upon how much it is allowed to thicken.

Rhubarb Crunch

2 recipes graham cracker
  crust
3 cups diced rhubarb

1/2 cup sugar
1 teaspoon salt
1 teaspoon cinnamon

Pat half the pastry into a 9- x 13- x 2-inch pan. Combine the rest of ingredients and spoon over pastry. Spread the rest of the pastry over top. Bake at 350°F. for forty-five to fifty minutes. Serve warm with whipped or ice cream.

SPINACH

Spinach Loaf

2 cups cooked chopped spinach
1/2 cup tomato sauce or
  ketchup
1 cup bread crumbs

1 onion, minced
1 teaspoon salt
3 hard-cooked eggs

Mix all ingredients except eggs. Place half of mixture in greased loaf pan. Lay hard-cooked eggs straight up middle (the long way, in a row). Pour rest of ingredients over eggs. Bake at 350°F. for about thirty minutes. When slicing, each slice will have a nice chunk of hard-cooked egg in the center. Good because it can be prepared earlier and heated when ready to serve. *Serves 6-8.*

Spinach and Potatoes

1/2 cup cooked chopped spinach
1 medium potato, mashed

Salt
Pepper

Mix and mash together spinach and potato. Add salt and pepper to taste. May be served as potato and vegetable with meat. *Serves 1.*

Serving suggestion:
Prepare a fried egg. Place atop mixture. Serve in individual ramekin or serving dish. Delicious lunch for child or adult.

Spinach with Walnuts and Raisins

2-3 pounds spinach	1/8 teaspoon pepper
1/2 cup raisins	2 tablespoons butter or mar-
1/2 cup chopped walnuts	garine
1 teaspoon salt	

Wash spinach and drain. Put in large pot. Cover. Do not add any water. Steam about ten minutes. Pour off liquid. Add raisins, nuts, salt and pepper. Stir and mix to heat through. Place in serving dish. Dot with butter. *Serves 4.*

Spinach Salad

2 pounds spinach	1 teaspoon salt
1 onion, minced	1/4 teaspoon freshly ground
1 tablespoon oil	pepper
1 cup plain yogurt	1 clove garlic

Wash spinach. Tear into bite-sized pieces; do not add water. Cook only in water which clings to spinach. Add onion. Cook three minutes. Drain. Add oil. Cook two more minutes. Remove from heat; cool. Add yogurt, salt, pepper and garlic. Stir gently, remove garlic and serve. *Serves 3-4.*

Creamed Spinach

2 tablespoons butter	Pepper
2 cups cooked finely chopped	1 tablespoon flour
spinach	1/2 cup hot milk (or cream)
1 finely minced onion	Nutmeg
Salt	

Melt butter in saucepan. Put finely chopped spinach into saucepan. Add onion, salt and pepper. Stir flour in and mix about two minutes. Slowly add and mix milk (or cream). Cook only about two minutes. Remove from saucepan, pour into serving dish and sprinkle with nutmeg. Same recipe may be used with other greens (such as Swiss chard). *Serves 4-5.*

Spinach Luncheon

1 pound ground beef	1/8 teaspoon pepper
2 minced onions	2 pounds spinach, washed, drained and torn into bite-size pieces
1 teaspoon salt	

Brown beef in large skillet. Stir and add onions and seasoning. Add spinach. Cover and simmer about ten minutes. Serve over toast triangles with sliced fresh cucumbers and tomatoes. *Serves 4.*

SQUASH
My Favorite Baked Squash

2 butternut or acorn squash	1/2 teaspoon cinnamon
2 teaspoons sugar	Butter or margarine

Wash and cut squash in half lengthwise. Remove seeds and any stringy fiber. Sprinkle with sugar and cinnamon mixture. Put a dab of butter in each squash. Place in baking pan and bake at 350°F. for about one hour or until tender. Add a little water to pan as it bakes to prevent pan from scorching. *Serves 4.*

Pot Pourri

2 tablespoons vegetable oil	1 cup diced potatoes
1 cup chopped squash	1 medium onion, minced
1 cup chopped tomatoes	3/4 teaspoon salt
1 cup cooked corn	Dash pepper
1/2 cup diced green pepper	Oregano

Warm vegetable oil. Add all ingredients except oregano. Cover and simmer thirty minutes. Add oregano. Mix and serve. If you wish, add anything else that happens to be ripe and available. *Serves 6-8.*

Stuffed Squash

Almost any variety of squash may be used, provided the size will suit your purpose. Wash, cut in half and either bake or steam until tender. Scoop out inside, leaving about one-half inch of squash within the skin. Gently and quickly sauté ground beef (add salt and pepper to taste), add diced onion, diced green pepper, (about one-half cup cooked rice if you have some left over) and the squash. Stir until beef is cooked and vegetables tender but still crisp. Spoon mixture into squash "shells" and keep warm in low oven while serving first course. Bread crumbs or Parmesan cheese may be sprinkled over the top just before placing in oven.

Simple Squash Stew

1 pound ground beef	1/2 cup diced green pepper
1 cup chopped squash	1 tablespoon margarine or
1/2 cup diced eggplant	butter
1 onion	

Gently sauté all ingredients in melted margarine. Season with salt and pepper to taste. Be sure not to overcook vegetables. Put individual portions into individual pyrex dishes (we use the one-pint size). Sprinkle with bread crumbs or Parmesan cheese or both, depending upon who likes what. Put into oven to keep warm until ready for main course. Delightful served with cold sliced tomatoes and crisp cucumbers. *Serves 4.*

TOMATOES

Tomato Conserve

3 pounds tomatoes	2 cups sugar
1/4 ounce ginger root or pre-served ginger	1 lemon, thinly sliced

Cook tomatoes for forty-five minutes. At same time cut ginger root finely and boil ten minutes in a separate pot using fresh water. When tomatoes have cooked, add sugar, lemon and cooked ginger root. Cook until thick and smooth. Pour into sterilized jars and seal. If preserved ginger is used, just slice and add to conserve while cooking. *Yield: 4-5 1/2 pints.*

Your Very Own Tomato Sauce

3 very large ripe tomatoes (or
   about 2 1/2 pounds of
   whatever variety is ripe at
   the time)
1/2 green pepper
1 medium onion

2 celery ribs
2 1/2 tablespoons melted butter
2 tablespoons brown sugar
1/4 teaspoon paprika
3/4 teaspoon salt

Wash, core, cut and mash tomatoes. Place in large saucepan.
Dice very finely: pepper, onion and celery. Simmer about forty-
five minutes. Use a double boiler so you don't have to stir. Put
tomato mix through food mill or sieve. Return to pot. Add all
other ingredients and simmer thirty minutes more. *Yield: about
2 cups.* This recipe has been doubled and tripled very successfully, and canned.

Open-Faced Tomato Cheese Sandwich

White bread
Ripe tomatoes
American cheese slices
Salt

Pepper
Parmesan cheese
Oregano

Toast bread. On each slice of toast place one slice of American
cheese and one slice of tomato (about 1/2 inch thick). Salt and
pepper, Parmesan cheese and oregano should then be sprinkled
on. Place on cookie sheet and heat under broiler until Parmesan
cheese melts.

If You Must Broiled Tomatoes

Ripe tomatoes
Salt
Pepper

Bread crumbs
Parmesan cheese

Cut ripe tomatoes in 1/2-inch slices. Season with salt and
pepper. Place on cookie sheet. Sprinkle with bread crumbs and
Parmesan cheese. Place under broiler until cheese melts.

Tomatoes in Sour Cream

1 1/2 cups bread crumbs	1/4 teaspoon pepper
4 large tomatoes	1 teaspoon sugar
1 onion	1 cup sour cream
4 teaspoons salt	

Place one-third of bread crumbs in greased, square baking dish. Slice tomatoes and onion. Place one layer of tomatoes and few slices of onion in dish. Mix salt, pepper and sugar. Sprinkle some over tomatoes. Repeat one-third of bread crumbs, then tomatoes, etc., until tomatoes are used up. Pour sour cream over tomatoes and cover with remaining bread crumbs. Bake at 375°F. for one hour. *Serves 5-6.* To tell the truth this didn't go over too well in our house—we prefer our tomatoes fresh, raw and cold.

Greek Salad

3 diced tomatoes	1 green or red pepper, diced
3 diced carrots	1/2 cup diced green olives
1 diced cucumber	1/2 cup diced black olives

Mix and toss all ingredients. Greek cheese or bits of raw herring may be added if desired. French dressing may be poured over top. Toss and serve. *Serves 7-8.*

ZUCCHINI

Zucchini Salad

4 zucchini	1 small cucumber
2 tomatoes	2 tablespoons mayonnaise
1 green pepper	2 tablespoons French dressing
1 onion (optional)	

Wash and prepare all vegetables. Peel cucumber. Chop. Put into serving bowl. Toss. Add salt and pepper. Mix together mayonnaise and French dressing. Toss, mix and serve immediately. *Serves 6.*

Stuffed Zucchini

2 medium zucchini	1/8 teaspoon pepper
1 pound ground beef	3/4 cup cooked rice
1 medium onion, minced	1 cup tomato sauce
Vegetable oil	2 tablespoons brown sugar
1 teaspoon salt	Juice of 1 lemon

Cut zucchini in half the long way. Scoop out zucchini, leaving a three-quarter-inch shell. Sauté the diced scooped-out squash, ground beef and the minced onion in vegetable oil. Season and simmer about fifteen minutes. Add cooked rice, stir and simmer ten minutes more. Pack lightly into shells. Place in baking pan. Combine final three ingredients. Pour over zucchini. Bake at 350°F. about one hour or until tender. *Serves 4.*

SPECIAL RECIPES
THAT COMBINE
MANY VEGETABLES

Garden Medley

Zucchini	1 teaspoon salt
Eggplant	1/8 teaspoon pepper
Tomatoes	1/2 teaspoon garlic powder
Peppers	1/2 teaspoon oregano
Onions	Basil
Mushrooms	Tomato paste

As you can see this is a "use whatever is in season that you like" recipe. Scrub but do not peel vegetables. Heat a little vegetable oil in a deep pot. Add vegetables, cut in bite-size chunks, seasonings and tomato paste. Simmer until all vegetables are tender but still crisp and until amost all liquid is absorbed. Serve as a hot vegetable; as a filling for an omelet; or chilled (mashed) and served on crackers as an appetizer.

Garden Spanish Omelet

2 eggs	1/4 cup chopped tomato
1 tablespoon water	1/4 cup chopped green pep-
Pinch salt	per
Pinch thyme	1 teaspoon chopped chives
Pinch parsley	

In small bowl mix eggs and water, add salt, thyme and parsley. Set aside. Put one tablespoon butter in small skillet. When melted add tomato, green pepper and chives. Sauté on low flame about five mintues. Heat omelet pan. Put in one tablespoon butter and heat until foamy. Add eggs. Stir with fork until set. Lower heat and cook until soft set. Make sure omelet is movable in pan. When omelet is finished spoon tomato mixture over one-half of omelet. Fold in half and slide immediately onto warm plate. *Serves 1.*

Tuna Salad

1 small head lettuce	2 strips celery
2 large tomatoes	1 green or red pepper
1 medium cucumber	1 7-ounce can tuna
2 carrots	2 hard-cooked eggs

Wash and tear lettuce into bite-size pieces. Put into large serving bowl. Wash and cut tomatoes, cucumbers, carrots and celery into bite-size pieces. Clean and dice green pepper. Add to lettuce. Add drained, flaked tuna. Mix thoroughly. Chop eggs, sprinkle over top and serve. Salad may be eaten plain or with dressing of your choice. *Serves 4.*

Delightful Diet Dip

1 pound cottage cheese	2 tablespoons skimmed milk
1 green pepper (cleaned and diced)	

Put all ingredients into blender. Blend until smooth. Salt if desired. Use as a dip or on toast.

Barbara's Burgers
Do-It-Yourself Barbecue Dinner

Barbecue hamburgers (if you can buy oversized hamburger buns do so, and make the burgers extra size to fit). Arrange on separate platters: sliced tomatoes, sliced cucumber, sliced onion, sliced green pepper and shredded lettuce. Have small, individual bowls of ketchup, mayonnaise, relish, pickle and dressing. Give each person a burger on a bun then—they're on their own. Everyone makes his own combination. Remember to serve dampened face cloths for mopping up—burgers are *very* messy to eat.

Garden Sandwich

Extra thin sliced bread   Sliced tomatoes
Sliced cucumbers   Hard-cooked eggs

Place one slice of bread on plate. Place cucumber slices on top. Cover with second slice of bread. Slice egg and place on sandwich. Cover with third slice of bread. Put sliced tomato on next. Cover with fourth slice of bread. Use dressing and/or seasonings to taste.

Horty's Chinese Pepper Steak

1 1/2 to 2 pounds round steak   1 1/2 ounces soy sauce
  or shoulder steak   1 can bean sprouts (drained)
2-3 green peppers, sliced   1/4 cup white cooking wine
Garlic powder   1 cup boiling water
Pepper   1/2 cup mushrooms
1 envelope beef bouillon pow-   2 tablespoons oil
  der

Brown meat in oil in large heavy skillet. Add all ingredients. Cook about fifteen minutes (until peppers are tender but still crisp). Add a little more boiling water if necessary. Cover and cook about 1 1/2 hours (until meat is tender). Serve with rice and Chinese noodles. *Serves 6.*

Riviera Appetizer

2 medium tomatoes
1 cucumber (6 inches long)
6 hard-cooked eggs
French dressing

Russian dressing
1/4 cup minced chives
1 green or red pepper, diced

Wash and slice tomatoes (1/2 inch thick). Peel cucumber. Hold cucumber in flat of hand. With other hand run fork down length of cucumber cutting into flesh. Continue to do this around entire cucumber. When sliced this produces an attractive effect. Slice cucumbers on an angle (1/2 inch thick) making an oval-shaped slice. Cut eggs in half lengthwise. Place one slice cucumber and one slice tomato side by side on cake plate. Place 1/2 of hard-cooked egg (cut side down) on each. Spoon French dressing carefully over one half and Russian dressing over the other. Garnish with chives and pepper. Serve immediately with small salted crackers. *Serves 6.*

Carol's Gazpacho

2 large tomatoes, peeled
1 large cucumber, peeled and
   halved ›
1 medium onion
1 green pepper
32 ounces tomato juice

1/3 cup olive oil
1/3 cup red wine vinegar
1/8 teaspoon Worces-
   tershire sauce
1 1/2 teaspoons salt
1/8 teaspoon pepper

In electric blender, combine tomatoes, one-half cucumber, one-half onion, one-half green pepper and one-half cup tomato juice. Blend, covered, at high speed to puree vegetables. In a large bowl mix the puree with the remaining tomato juice, one-third cup olive oil, vinegar, Worcestershire sauce and seasonings. Refrigerate covered mixture for a few hours. Refrigerate serving bowls. Dice remaining vegetables. Put each in a small separate bowl. (May serve croutons too.) Serve soup and let everyone add his own diced vegetables. *Serves 6-8.*

Garden Kebabs

2 pounds beef, veal or lamb   18 small cooked onions
(or any combination), cut in   18 cherry tomatoes
bite-size pieces   18 large mushrooms
2 large green peppers, cut in
bite-size chunks

Spear foods, in order, on skewers. Season and grill. They may be brushed with homemade ketchup, barbecue or tomato sauce. They may be broiled indoors or grilled outdoors. Turn often to prevent burning. *Serves 6.*

CHAPTER 5

Fruits and
Berries and Love

EVERYONE WHO HAS a small piece of ground owes himself the joy and the pleasure of growing his own fruits and berries. The city dweller with the pathetically small backyard, the suburbanite who figures in fractions of acres and the country gentleman and "almost" farmer all can grow some of these wonderful plants. Nothing any of these home gardeners (either experienced or novice) can grow will give them more enjoyment with less work, better value at less cost or greater all around beauty and utility, than fruits and berries.

Though some may classify them differently, for our purposes we use "fruits" to mean those grown on trees like apples, cherries, peaches, pears and plums. Anything that grows on bushes or vines we call berries, including blackberries, blueberries, currants, elderberries, gooseberries, huckleberries, raspberries and grapes. We keep strawberries and melons (cantaloupe, Persian and cranshaw plus several varieties of watermelon) in separate categories because we grow them in and around the vegetable garden.

One general rule applies to all the fruits and berries—though they require relatively little care and attention, the small amount they demand must be met or your harvest will suffer. A little bit of TLC and you'll have beautiful trees, bushes and vines with magnificent blossoms and delicious fruits and berries. Let's see the kind of care and attention required to successfully grow fruit trees.

Perhaps the greatest amount of care and attention should be paid before you own a single fruit tree. For example, proper fruit tree selection can mean the difference between a good crop, a poor crop and no crop at all. Often it can mean the difference between life and death for the tree.

Start checking into fruit trees by going to a local, well-known nursery or looking through the catalogs of the better-known mail-order nurserymen. Deal only with reputable, reliable nurserymen. There are few bargains in fruit trees so expect the old adage, "you get what you pay for," to hold true. Spend a fair price at a reliable nursery and be certain you are investing in the best, strongest, straightest, healthiest trees.

Whether you buy locally or order through a mail-order catalog you must first determine certain facts if you are to have any success. Will the kind and variety of tree you have chosen be suited to your area's temperature and rainfall conditions? Too little rainfall in some areas and too short summers in others will just about guarantee failure of the trees to produce fruit. Select only those trees and those varieties recommended for your area.

Another consideration is the size of the tree at maturity. Will the tree or trees get so big they will overpower your property and leave little or no room for other plantings and activities? If this possibility is going to force you to pass up fruit trees, consider the wonderful dwarf fruit trees available in most parts of the country. In many ways these dwarf trees are ideal for the new gardener, the new homeowner and the small property owner. They are considerably smaller than standard trees but produce full-sized fruit. They require less time and attention to maintain and care for, and are much easier to pick (no ladder, merely stretch out your arm and pick clean). Additional good news to the new and enthusiastic gardener is that they bear one and sometimes two years earlier than standard-size trees. Dwarfs can also be used to serve double and triple duty. Not only are they prized for the taste and quality of fruit they deliver in a very small area, but they are also used as decorative and specimen trees in a landscaping plan (they have beautiful blossoms, marvelous shape and fantastic leaf color), and as espaliered trees in various shapes for various purposes.

In defense of the larger trees, you will find they are less expensive to buy, they live and bear fruit a bit longer than the dwarfs and produce a much larger crop (for example, a dwarf apple tree will yield two bushels to six for the standard-size tree). To round out the comparison, the larger trees can often serve double duty as magnificent shade and ornamental trees. Don't sit under one in the fall when it's windy or you'll prove Newton's law all over again.

A further consideration when selecting fruit trees concerns pollination. Some fruit trees will be loaded with blossoms but will bear little if any fruit. Others will be loaded with blossoms and then be loaded with fruit. The reason for this is that some trees, called self-fruitful, can pollinate their own blossoms and bear fruit. These trees do not require other varieties of the same fruit for pollination. On the other hand, self-unfruitful varieties must be planted near other varieties of the same fruit if the trees are to bear fruit. When deciding on the varieties of trees for your home, be sure to check the varieties against a pollination chart and then buy and plant those varieties that assure you of proper pollination of all the trees. If a neighbor (a very close neighbor, like a next-door neighbor) has the same type of trees, but other varieties, they may help pollinate your trees. Remember, apples will only pollinate apples, peaches only peaches, etc.

To give yourself the best chance to get fruit from whatever fruit trees and varieties you select, follow some simple guidelines. Plant at least two, and preferably more, apple varieties near to each other on your property. Some sweet cherries will not pollinate each other, so if you have Bing, Lambert, Napoleon or Black Tartarian in mind, plan on putting another variety in with any of them. Some sour cherry varieties can be planted by themselves, especially Montmorency. Peaches need no help and can be planted by themselves. Pears and plums require cross-pollination so don't buy just one variety and expect to harvest fruit. At least two different pear varieties and two different plum varieties are required for pollination that results in fruit.

Double-check with the man from whom you buy your fruit trees on hardiness, size and pollination. He's in the best position to know the area in which you live and the requirements of the trees he has for sale. Most trees bought at the nursery will be balled and burlapped (a soil ball surrounding the tree's roots are dug as a unit, wrapped in burlap and tied), or grown in large containers (including tin cans, plastic tubs or organic pots). In both cases there is a considerable amount of soil around the roots to protect them and keep them moist. Some trees bought at the nursery and almost all trees bought through the mail come bare root—that is, with no soil, just some moist peat moss or other moist packing material around the roots. Although there is much pro and con concerning the best way to dig and ship fruit trees, one conclusion is certain. Handled properly, trees packed in any of these three ways will do well. Those packed with soil surrounding the roots take a little less time getting used to their surroundings.

Whichever way they arrive home, young trees should be cared for as soon as possible. All should be planted almost immediately after they arrive at your home. If immediate planting of soil-packed trees is impossible, put the trees into a cool, windless spot and water the root ball frequently. If you allow the ball to dry out the chances are you'll kill the tree. Bare-root trees require even more careful attention to a few details if they are to survive until planting time.

On arrival at your home, open all packages and check the packing materials and the roots for dryness. If there is any hint of dryness, soak the packing materials and the roots in a tub of water for several hours. If it is still too soon to plant the trees, "heel them in" until you are ready. This is a temporary kind of planting designed to keep the roots and the tree in good shape until you can plant it in its final place. Simply dig a shallow V-shaped trench in a shaded area of your property. Lay the tree's roots, still covered by the moist packaging material, into the trench and cover with soil. Water as often as necessary to keep the roots from drying out and plant as soon as possible in its final location.

Planting time is another of those items that can start a discussion just as soon as two or more gardeners get together. As far as we can tell, the best time to plant trees is early spring, with late fall and early winter holding the runner-up positions. Though planting time is not nearly as critical for balled-and-burlapped trees as it is for bare-root trees, it is a good idea to get all trees into the ground as soon as possible after their arrival.

Start the tree-planting ceremony by checking your landscaping plan to be certain you have found the correct spot. Check and double-check everything at this time—trees cannot be redug and moved at your whim and fancy. Find a spot, make sure it is the correct spot and prepare to plant each tree to stay. Mark off a circle that is roughly twice the size of the roots or root ball. Then start digging. Cover the surrounding area with heavy paper, tarpaulin or a heavy duty plastic drop cloth to hold the soil you take out of the hole. The coverings will also keep you from messing up a large part of your lawn. If for one reason or another hole digging is not "your thing" many nurseries will plant the trees you buy from them adding only a small labor charge.

Dig the hole approximately twice as deep and twice as large across as the roots are when spread out or twice the size of the root ball. Refill about one-quarter of the hole with a mixture of compost, top soil and well-rotted or dehydrated manure. At this point the procedure for planting bare root fruit trees differs a bit from that of fruit trees with soil surrounding the roots.

When planting a bare-root fruit tree, always keep the roots covered (with peat moss or packing material) and never let them dry out. In most cases if you allow the roots to dry out you can save yourself the trouble of planting the tree—it is either dead or dying. If at all possible, do your hole-digging early in the day and do the actual planting late in the day when the sun is going down and it is not windy. Both sun and wind can quickly dry out tree roots.

In the bottom of the large hole you've dug, build a small mound of topsoil. Spread the bare roots over and all around the mound. If any roots are torn or damaged, cut them off. Quickly check the depth of the tree. Standard-size trees should be planted one to two inches deeper than they were at the nursery. Dwarf trees must be planted with the grafting knob two inches above the surface of the soil. Lay your shovel handle across the hole and use it as a guide to find the correct depth of the tree. Get the tree's depth and position correctly (be sure it is turned and facing the way you like it best) and start refilling the hole.

First back into the hole should be first out of the hole. That is, the topsoil goes into the hole first followed by subsoil and sand to

The key to successful tree planting is in the hole. Dig holes twice the size of the root ball and mix compost and topsoil in the bottom for guaranteed results.

Balled-and-burlapped trees can be planted just as they come from the nursery. Burlap spread out in hole will rot and become part of the soil.

Young trees must be wrapped to prevent sun scald and staked until their roots "take hold." Saucer depression around tree will collect and aim water to where it will do the most good.

keep the richer soil closer to the roots. Mix compost, organic matter and well-rotted or dehydrated manure with all the soil as it goes back into the hole. After the first few shovelsful of soil have gone into the soil, check and see that there are no air pockets around the roots. Use your fingers to move in and around the roots and for soil-breaking and filling any air pockets that may exist. Allowed to remain they will dry roots and damage or kill the tree. Add some more soil, shake the tree gently so soil filters down around the roots, add more soil and tamp gently but firmly.

Most young fruit trees require staking for the first few years after transplanting, until their roots take firm hold. Before the hole is refilled, drive two stakes, opposite each other, into the outermost parts of the hole. Doing this with the hole still half-filled allows you to see 'where the stakes are going and prevents your putting them through any of the root system. After the hole has been filled, hold the tree to the stake with wire. Protect the tree by slipping the wire that comes in contact with the trunk through a piece of plastic or rubber hose.

Continue to add soil to the hole until it reaches a level about two inches below normal ground level. Tamp the soil frequently and gently. When the job is done, the fruit tree should stand in the middle of a saucer-shaped circle. Fill the saucer with water and allow it to drain slowly into the ground. Repeat the process at least twice, adding soil to the saucer each time so the level remains constant. After the water has drained through the second time, fill the saucer almost to ground level with peat moss, grass clippings or other organic mulch. The slight depression that remains will catch and direct water to the tree's roots.

Balled-and-burlapped and container-grown trees are planted with the soil ball intact. Lift the ball and place it into the hole that has been one-quarter refilled with compost, top soil and dehydrated manure. Always pick these trees up by the ball, never by the trunk. Once the balled tree is in the hole, cut away the string that holds the burlap to the ball. Open the burlap and spread it out flat, all around the hole. The burlap will rot in time and will not inhibit the tree's root growth. Add soil and tamp firmly. Follow the same planting suggestions given for bare root fruit trees.

Container-grown trees must be removed from their containers before planting unless they are growing in peat or other organic pots. Tin snips, used carefully, will do a good job on both tin cans and plastic pots, without damaging the tree's roots. Before trying to cut through the container, try to remove the tree from the container as you would a much smaller plant from, for example, a clay pot.

Wet the soil thoroughly. Stop watering when the soil is wet and solid and just before it turns muddy. Get a good grip on the tree's trunk and turn the tree upside down so the soil in the top (open end) of the can rests on your hand. Give the bottom of the can a solid rap with a rock or a hammer and it should free the root ball. Discard the container and plant the tree as you would a balled-and-burlapped tree.

Once the trees have been planted and staked they are pretty much on their own. The few things remaining for you to do for them are very important. All are designed to get your tree acclimated to its new environment with the least amount of shock.

Immediately after planting, wrap the tree's trunk from soil line to the first major lateral branch with tree-wrap paper. This paper will prevent the sun from scalding the tender outer layer of the trunk and will also dissuade domestic and small wild animals from nibbling. Allow the paper to remain on the tree for at least one year and don't worry about stunting the tree's growth. The paper will expand as the tree grows and the trunk becomes thicker.

Watering, too, is very important for the young fruit tree. If there has not been a considerable rainfall at least once during the week, soak the saucer and surrounding area thoroughly with a soaker hose or bubble attachment for your hose.

Do not feed your trees the first year. They must become established before the fertilizer can do any good. After the first year add quantities of compost, organic materials and well-rotted manure and the tree will take care of itself.

As in the case of vegetables and other grown eatables, you must protect your fruit trees from diseases and insects. This can become a problem if all the people around you are filling the air with a full range of insecticides, miticides and fungicides, driving everything to your property. The most important single thing you can do is to keep your trees healthy and thriving so they can ward off insects and diseases. Keep the trees and the area in which they grow as clean as possible. Keep the area mulched down and remove all materials that are diseased or might breed disease. Follow a spraying program as outlined in Chapter 2 for vegetables which calls for the use of various methods and organic materials. Try each in turn and experiment until you find the material or combination that does the job for you. The effort is more than repaid when you can go into your "orchard" and pick and eat a piece of fruit without also getting a mouthful of poison.

Speaking of picking fruit, don't expect to pick any the first or second year. It takes a bit longer than that so check the specific fruit suggestions that follow for additional information.

APPLES—Will bear after about four years and continue to do so for about 50 years. Dwarf apples like most other dwarfs will bear about one year earlier, but may not bear for the full bearing period of a standard tree. Allow apples to ripen on the tree and then pick and eat, make into sauce, pies and other treats. To store put in a slotted bushel basket and keep in cool dry spot.

Try to pick apples and all other fruits so the stem comes off the tree and remains with the fruit. Intact in this way the fruit will keep in storage better. When the stem is pulled out of the fruit and left on the tree the hole left in the fruit is an open invitation to insects and spoilage. After harvesting, always use the fruit without stems first.

There are so many excellent apple varieties it is almost impossible to make a choice. Instead, sample some of the apples grown in your area in orchards, friends' backyards and anywhere else and decide on the variety you prefer. Decide also if you want them for eating as they come from the tree, or for cooking in sauces or pies, or anything else that comes to mind. Some excellent eating varieties are McIntosh, Red and Yellow De- licious, Baldwin and Winesap. Apples that are superb in sauces and pies include Rhode Island Greening, Northern Spy, Cort- land, York, Rome Beauty, Lobo and Milton.

CHERRIES—Take your pick of these for you can have both sweet and sour cherries according to your taste. That is, when fully ripe, some cherries are quite sweet while other varieties are quite sour. If you live in a very cold area stick to the sour cherries. They are considerably hardier than the sweet varieties.

Sweet cherry trees will start bearing three years after planting.

Though it looks ghost-like this gauze-wrapped cherry tree will produce many, many delicious cherries. Without the protection of the gauze, the birds and not you will have the feast.

Sour cherries take a year longer, but will live and bear for at least 50 years or about 20 years longer than sweet cherries. To protect your ripening cherries from the birds, throw a gauze net over the entire tree. If you don't do this the birds will literally eat the cherries right off the tree and leave you a clean pit suspended from the stem. You'll be lucky if you have a handful to eat.

Some fine sweet cherry varieties are Bing, Napoleon, Lambert and Black Tartarian. Early Richmond and Montmorency are the best sour cherries.

PEACHES—Though they are the most popular fruit grown in the United States, peaches only do well in the warmer parts of the country. If the temperature in your area gets down about 10° to 15°F. below zero, don't try to grow peaches. If there is any doubt about your temperature and you have planted peach trees, protect them as best you can with antidessicant spray, burlap, sheeted plastic and anything else you have at hand.

Allow peaches to ripen on the tree, but pick just as soon as they start to ripen and there is a bit of give when you apply finger pressure to the skin. Peach trees will bear about three years after planting and will continue to give a full crop for at least ten years. When the crop starts to decline from year to year it is time to replant a few trees each year.

Some excellent peach varieties include Elberta, Golden Jubilee, Belle of Georgia and Carman.

PEARS—One of the most delightful of the dessert fruits, pears are usually relatively easy to grow, but are susceptible to blights and must be watched carefully. Do not allow pears to ripen on the tree. When they have reached full size, but are not ripe, pick them carefully off the tree. Snap off the stem so part remains intact in the fruit. Wrap the fruit in tissue paper and store until ripe in a warm (about 68° F.), dry spot. Will bear three years after planting and continue to bear for almost fifty years or as long as they are cared for and kept healthy.

Some of the better known and thoroughly enjoyed varieties include Anjou, Bartlett, Bosc, Clapp's Favorite, Comice and Seckel.

PLUMS—These wonderful fruits come in various sizes, shapes and colors. If they are to be eaten raw as a dessert fruit, they

The tree is small but the crop is big when dwarf pear trees start producing. When pears reach full size, but before they are ripe, pick them and bring them inside for ripening.

should be allowed to tree ripen. If they are for canning they should be a trifle harder, picked just before they are ripe enough to eat raw. Because there are two distinct types of plums, European and Japanese, that will not pollinate each other, check carefully when you buy or you may end up with beautiful trees and no fruit.

Plums will bear after about four years and will continue, if cared for, for about twenty to twenty-five years.

Fine European plums include Reine Claude, Italian Prune and Green Gage. Japanese plums include Abundance, Santa Rosa and Formosa.

If you have no room for the larger fruits you certainly should find room for berries. Everyone should be able to place at least one or two bushes or vines. Remember, too, that many of these bushes can be used as ornamentals, as fences or as screens, doing double-duty.

All of the buying, planting, fertilizing and watering suggestions listed for the large fruits also apply to these small fruits. Except in very, very windy areas, the small bushes require no staking. As you plan for small fruits be sure to read the specific suggestions that follow for special growing requirements.

BLACKBERRIES—A part of the bramble family that includes raspberries, blackberries are very highly thought of, but frequently ignored by home gardeners. Plants should be set out in the spring, three feet apart in rows that are at least eight feet apart. Plant only in well-fertilized soil that is full of organic matter because the plants will grow and multiply within this area. Brambles send out healthy shoots the first year and berries the second year. Many people use a trellis or vine arrangement to keep the long, branched stalks from becoming tangled and making the area virtually impassable.

Do not prune blackberries the first year. The second year, cut back the new canes to about 30 inches so branching will take place. Mulch the area around the plants with a layer of organic material that is at least three inches thick. If new shoots are desired for additional plants, move the mulch away in the spring and respread again when the shoots are up.

Brambles require frequent watering during the hottest part of the summer for that is when their crops mature. Mulching helps to retain a lot of water in the soil, but you should plan to water several times each week after fruit has set and starts to ripen. Blackberries are self-fruitful and so only one variety need be grown. They will continue to grow fruit indefinitely—or as long as they are cared for and cultivated.

Recommended varieties include Ebony King, Eldorado and Midnight.

RASPBERRIES—A close cousin to the blackberry, this group includes red, black and purple varieties. One difference between raspberries and blackberries becomes evident at harvest time—raspberries when ripe are detached from their core while blackberries are eaten core and all.

Cultivated and grown the same way as the other brambles, raspberries do best in the cooler climates. When planting, cut back the stalks to about one foot and set plants several inches deeper into the soil than they were at the nursery.

Red raspberries must be pruned every year. Cut out all old canes immediately after fruit has been picked. Cut the remainder of the canes to between 30 and 36 inches tall. Black raspberries are pruned differently. First, pinch the shoot tips off when the stalks are about two feet long. After all fruit has been picked, prune the second time by removing all old canes. Late in the winter, cut back side shoots so they stand no taller than about one foot.

Some recommended varieties of red raspberries include: Latham, Milton and September; for black ones: Bristol and Cumberland; for purple ones: Sodus and Columbian.

BLUEBERRIES—Grown on bushes, these berries are relatively new to the home garden, but they are a welcome addition. Sometimes huckleberries are called blueberries and vice versa; the only real difference being that huckleberries have much harder seeds than true blueberries.

Strong, two-year-old bushes should be planted in the spring about six to eight feet apart each way. If a beautiful, fruit-bearing hedge or fence is desired, the bushes can be planted considerably closer together. Plant only in well-fertilized soil that is definitely quite acid (pH about 4.5) and contains large amounts of organic matter.

Blueberries rarely yield fruit the first year, but the second year the fruits are large and the crop heavy. Because blueberries are very shallow-rooted, mulching is important. If mulch is not used, all weeding must be done by hand for tools may cut the roots close to the soil's surface.

Watering all during the time the berries are developing is important or the crop will be smaller and considerably less plump. Fertilizer, too, should be spread around the bushes, but be sure it is kept about six inches away from any of the plant's branches.

Pruning is vital to blueberries despite the fact that it reduces the total crop. It more than makes up for this by greatly increasing the size and quality of the individual berries. Prune out all old wood and all weak, thin branches once a year, preferably when the bush is dormant—between November and March. With this kind of careful pruning you will have lots of large, juicy berries and lots and lots of birds. Cover the plants with netting or you'll have few blueberries left for yourself.

Harvest the berries when they are completely blue except if you are making jam or jelly. Red-tinted berries mixed in with ripe blueberries eliminate the need for pectin in jelly- and jam-making.

Recommended varieties are Earliblue, Ivanhoe and Rancocas.

GOOSEBERRIES—Another one of the neglected small fruits, gooseberries are excellent in jam, jelly and pie. Grown on small plants, gooseberries take up little room and yield a great many berries. Another small fruit, currants, are in the same family and have the same requirements.

Plant these small fruits in the fall or as early in the spring as the ground can be worked. They can be grown in most parts of the U. S., but they prefer cool summers if they are to set the best fruit. Space the plants about five feet apart each way when setting into well-fertilized, organic-material-rich soil. Mulch, water and fertilize as you would for other small fruits.

Pruning for both gooseberries and currants starts when the bushes are about three years old and is concerned mainly with the removal of old, dead or thin branches. If the bushes become too dense, some of the older canes can be removed to allow room for new, young canes.

Recommended varieties of currants include White Grape

(white fruit), Champion (black fruit) and Red Lake and Wilder (red fruit). Gooseberry selections include Poorman and Chautauqua.

GRAPES—Grown since earliest recorded history, grapes should have a place in your home landscaping plans. Figure to put your grapes in a place that is protected because they are quite susceptible to frost. Plant either in fall or very early spring in soil that has been enriched with large amounts of fertilizer and organic material. Set the plants about eight feet apart in straight rows that can later be tied to a trellis. Grapes will grow and bear for as long as 75 years so the soil around the plants should be continually fed with organic fertilizer.

When the vines are long enough they should be trained onto the trellis. Keep the vines spaced so there is always plenty of air between them allowing the sun through and limiting disease. Mulch all around the plants and throw some mulch around the trellis supports to keep down weed growth.

Some grapes are good for wine; others are good for eating; and still others are excellent in jams and jellies. Check on these qualities with your nurseryman and also ask about the varieties that are best suited to climate and rainfall conditions in your area.

Especially fine blue varieties include the famous Concord, as well as Steuben and Van Buren. Niagara is the premium white grape, and Agwam, Caco and Delaware are recommended red varieties.

STRAWBERRIES—There are so many reasons why strawberries are one of the favorite small fruits in the home garden that simply listing them would take pages and pages. It is enough to mention that they are the first fruit available in spring, they are delicious, good for you, take up little space and reward you with a large crop. How can you resist after all that?

Some strawberry varieties will grow under almost every climatic condition in the country, so select the right kind for your area. Soil condition, however, is very important. Strawberries only grow on soil that drains well. If water stands for any length of time on the spot you've selected for your strawberries, select another spot. Make sure the soil has been well-fertilized and is light rather than heavy and clay-like.

Though there are several different methods for planting strawberries, the matted row system seems best for home gardens. Put the plants about 1 1/2 feet apart in straight rows about 3 1/2 feet apart. As they grow, the plants will send out runners from which new plants will grow. Wherever the tip of the runner hits the open soil it will take root and you will have a new plant. If unattended, this would result in quite a mess—strawberry plants all over the place. In the matted row system, the runners are allowed to grow and new plants are allowed to start—if they are within the boundaries of the row. The row usually is about 1 1/2 to 2 feet wide and any runners that go outside the row are cut off. With this system, every once in a while, the plants are thinned so they stand about six inches apart from each other.

The initial planting of strawberry plants can be a bit tricky, though later on, nature does it all by herself with no trouble at all. The important parts of the planting procedure are: 1) the roots must be spread out in the hole and 2) the crown (the center of the plant where the small leaves develop) must be level with the soil's surface. Planted too high, the roots and crown will dry out.

One of the best planting procedures for strawberries involves two people. Start your planting on a cool, cloudy day. If it looks like rain, that's the day to plant strawberries. Mark out a straight line in the garden with a taut string. Take the unpacked strawberries (they should have been unpacked as soon as they arrived and kept, roots down, in a bucket of water) and separate them while they sit in the water bucket. The first person pushes his spade into the ground and when the entire blade is in the soil he pushes forward on the handle. This leaves a three- or four-inch space directly behind the spade blade. The second person inserts the strawberry plant, spreads out the roots and holds the crown so it is exactly at soil level. The spade man removes the tool and tamps the soil all around the plant. Move down about 18 inches and repeat the process. When all the plants have been set, water thoroughly, mulch and water again. Do not allow the newly set plants to dry out.

When blossoms appear the first year, pick them off so the plants become stronger instead of spending energy making berries. The second year you will have a fine crop of berries. Pick them during the cool part of the day and continue to pick every day or every other day until all are gone. Only allow people with large amounts of willpower to pick these luscious berries—everyone else will eat them right in the strawberry patch leaving none to bring into the house.

There are a great many different varieties of strawberries on the market with new ones being developed every year. Choose the variety best suited to your location. Some of the most highly recommended varieties include Earlidawn, Sparkle, Catskill, Surecrop. Of the everbearing varieties, Superfection and Gem are the most highly rated.

MELONS—These great big beauties, including Persian melon, cantaloupe, cranshaw melon and the various watermelons are really not fruits, but since most people think of them as such, here they are in the fruit section. For growing and other suggestions check the cucumber section in Chapter 2.

Now that you have all these magnificent fruits and berries growing in your garden or your "orchard," it's time to see some of the best ways to prepare and serve them. Hearty appetite!

APPLES
Applesauce

Apples   Cinnamon
Sugar

Wash and core apples. Do not peel. Cut into quarters or eighths. Put into large pot and add one cup of water. Cook until soft. (In a pressure cooker this takes about 2 minutes once the pressure is "up.") Put through food mill or sieve. You may add sugar and/or cinnamon to taste. The later in the season certain varieties (such as McIntosh) are picked, the sweeter they are—and often no sugar is needed at all. If you still have fresh peaches around, add two or three to the pot of apples before cooking—the result is a fantastic combination. Applesauce may be frozen if you do not have facilities for canning. However, we find that the flavor is not quite as good. Apples especially good for sauce and for pies include: Rome Beauty, McIntosh, Jonathan, Baldwin, Rhode Island Greening.

Applesauce Pie

Pour fresh, homemade applesauce into an unbaked 9″ pie shell. Cover with a second pastry shell slashed in several places with a lattice-type pastry cover, or cut out pastry designs with cookie cutters and arrange over the applesauce. Using cookie cutters for the pieces makes this (or any other) pie "special" for holidays or occasions. Bake in a preheated 450° F. oven for twenty minutes (until crust is nicely browned). Tastes even more interesting when served with sweet cream or topped with whipped cream.

Baked Apples

Large, perfect baking apples	1 tablespoon cinnamon
(Northern Spy, Rhode Island	Butter or margarine
Greening, Cortland, Rome	Water
Beauty or others)	Marshmallows (optional)
1/4 cup sugar	

Wash, core (do not go through to bottom of apple) and peel one inch of skin from top of apples. Mix sugar and cinnamon. Fill centers of apples with this mixture. Put a dab of butter on top of each. Put into shallow baking pan with one inch of boiling water. Cover with aluminum foil and bake about forty-five minutes at 375° F. Apples should be tender but *not* mushy. If desired, top with a tiny marshmallow. Baste several times with pan juices after removing from oven. Serve warm or cold, with sweet cream, if desired.

Apple Turnovers

1 recipe two-crust pastry	1/4 teaspoon nutmeg
2 cups sliced apples	1/4 cup raisins (or dates)
1/3 cup sugar	1/4 cup chopped walnuts
1 tablespoon flour	Melted shortening
1/4 teaspoon cinnamon	Sugar
	Cinnamon

Prepare pastry. Roll into ball and refrigerate until ready to roll. Combine all ingredients in medium-sized bowl. Roll out pastry to form a 9″ x 18″ rectangle. Cut into eight equal squares.

Put heaping tablespoon of filling on each square. Put it off to one side only, not in the middle. Using a pastry brush, moisten the four edges with water. Fold in half and seal by pressing tines of fork along edges. Fold to make either a rectangle or a triangle. Prick an A into top of each one, using the tines of a fork. Brush tops with melted shortening and sprinkle with sugar and cinnamon. Bake on cookie sheets about twenty minutes, until golden brown. Serve warm. These can be prepared in the morning, refrigerated and baked when ready to sit down for dinner. *Makes 8 turnovers.*

Apple Stuffing

4 cups diced, tart apples	1/2 teaspoon salt
1/4 cup butter or margarine	1/3 cup sugar
1/2 cup chopped onion	4 cups small bread cubes
1/2 cup chopped celery	

Melt shortening in a large skillet. Add all other ingredients except bread crumbs. Cook, stirring occasionally, for about ten minutes (apples should be lightly browned). Add bread crumbs. Toss lightly. *Yield: 4 cups.*

Nutty-Apple Butter Cookies

1/2 cup butter or margarine, softened at room temperature	1 teaspoon baking powder
	1/2 teaspoon salt
	1 cup apple butter
1/3 cup light brown sugar	1 cup rolled oats
2 eggs	1/2 cup chopped salted peanuts
1 cup sifted all-purpose flour	

Cream butter. Add light brown sugar and beat until fluffy. Add eggs one at a time, beating well after each addition. Sift together flour, baking powder and salt. Add creamed mixture and blend smooth. Add apple butter, rolled oats and mix thoroughly. Fold in chopped nuts. Drop by teaspoon about 1 1/2 inches apart, on greased baking sheets. Bake at 350°F. ten to twelve minutes. *Makes about six dozen cookies.*

Company Apple Breakfast Cake

7 cups sifted flour
1/4 cup baking powder
1 1/2 teaspoons salt
6 tablespoons sugar
1 cup shortening
3 beaten whole eggs

2 1/4 cups water
3 1/2 cups finely chopped apples
3 tablespoons melted butter
1 tablespoon plus 1 1/2 teaspoons cinnamon
1 2/3 cups sugar

Mix and sift flour, baking powder, salt and sugar into mixer bowl. Add shortening. Mix on low speed approximately one minute or until mixture resembles coarse corn meal. Add eggs and water. Mix until a soft dough is formed. Divide batter into two well-greased, 9- x-13-inch baking pans. Spread evenly. Combine apples, butter, cinnamon and sugar. Spread over batter in each pan. Bake at 400°F. approximately twenty-five minutes. *Yield: 25 portions.*

BERRIES

Blueberry Round Cake

2 tablespoons butter or margarine
3/4 cup sugar
1 egg
1 teaspoon vanilla

1 1/2 cups flour
2 teaspoons baking powder
1/2 cup milk
1 cup fresh blueberries

Cream butter and sugar. Add egg, mix well. Add vanilla. Sift together flour and baking powder. Add dry ingredients alternately with milk. Fold in blueberries. Bake in greased and floured 8-inch round cake pan, in 350°F. oven thirty to thirty-five minutes (until golden brown and cake tester comes out clean). Let cool for ten minutes, then invert on wire rack. Serve while still warm. This cake freezes very well, and should be put back into the oven (after completely defrosting) for ten minutes and served warm.

Blueberry Casserole Dessert

2 cups coarse bread crumbs (1/2 whole wheat and 1/2 white bread makes an interesting taste)
1/2 cup melted butter or margarine

4 cups fresh blueberries, washed and drained
2/3 cup brown sugar
2 tablespoons lemon juice

Toss bread crumbs with melted butter. Put a layer into a buttered casserole. Cover with layer of blueberries. Sprinkle with some brown sugar and lemon juice. Repeat until all ingredients are used up. Bake at 350°F. about forty minutes. If top gets too brown, cover with aluminum foil and continue baking. Serve at room temperature, topped with whipped cream or vanilla ice cream. *Serves 6.*

Quick Blueberry Tarts

4-5 cups blueberries
3/4 cup sugar

3/4 cup water
6 slices of white bread

Combine berries, sugar and water. Cook until soft. Remove bread crusts. Using rolling pin, roll each slice of bread until 1/2 the original thickness. Spread each side of slice with butter or margarine. Press one slice into 4-ounce pyrex dessert dish, shaping bread to fit dish. Fill dishes with blueberries. Bake at 350°F. about twenty minutes. Serve warm, topped with whipped cream or a small scoop of vanilla ice cream. *Serves 6.*

Gooseberry Sauce

1 pint fresh gooseberries (washed and drained)

1/2 cup superfine or confectioners' sugar

Place ingredients in blender. Blend five minutes. Serve over vanilla ice cream or pound cake. May be chilled or heated. *Yield: about 1 1/2 cups.*

Marilyn's Blueberry Cake

1/2 pound butter	4 teaspoons baking powder
2 cups sugar	1 teaspoon cinnamon
6 eggs	1 1/2 teaspoons vanilla
4 cups flour	1 quart ripe blueberries

Cream butter and sugar. Add eggs one at a time. Sift together flour, baking powder and cinnamon. Add vanilla. Add dry ingredients. Fold in blueberries. Grease 13- x 9- x 2-inch glass baking dish. (We haven't the courage to try to turn this cake out—too big. So we serve it right from the baking dish.) Bake at 350°F. for one hour.

Very Berry Pudding

1/2 cup shortening	3 teaspoons baking powder
3/4 cup sugar	1/2 teaspoon salt
1 cup milk	2 cups berries (mixed berries
1 egg	are excellent)
2 cups flour	

Cream shortening and sugar. Add milk and beaten egg. Sift together flour, baking powder and salt. Add and mix thoroughly. Fold in 2 cups berries. Pour into greased mold, then steam for one hour. (To steam without regular steamer, place mold into a deep kettle or pot filled about halfway with water. Count steaming time when water begins boiling. Add water if some cooks away.) Cool slightly, unmold and serve. *Yield: 4-6 servings.*

Huckleberry Dessert

1/2 cup sugar	1 1/2 cups sifted flour
1/3 cup margarine	1/2 cup milk
2 eggs	2 cups huckleberries

Cream sugar and shortening. Add eggs; mix well. Alternately add flour and milk. Grease bottom of 9-inch baking dish. Line with berries. Pour batter over berries. Bake at 375°F. for thirty-five minutes, until golden brown and cake tester comes out clean. *Serve cut in squares.*

Huckleberry Muffins

2 cups sifted flour	4 tablespoons melted short-
3 teaspoons baking powder	ening
3/4 teaspoon salt	3/4 cup milk
1/2 cup sugar	1 cup fresh huckleberries
2 eggs, beaten	

Sift together flour, baking powder, salt, sugar. Add eggs. Add shortening and milk. Fold in huckleberries. Fill well-greased muffin tins about two-thirds full. Bake in preheated oven at 400°F. twenty to twenty-five minutes. Allow to cool in tin about five minutes so they are easier to remove. Serve at once. Best when served fresh and hot. *Yield: 16-20 muffins.*

CHERRIES

Crunchy Cherry Dessert

2 cups pitted cherries (Bing, Lambert, Black Tartarian)	1 package yellow or white cake mix (1 layer)
	Margarine

Grease individual dessert cups. Place heaping tablespoon of cherries in cup. Sprinkle 2 level tablespoons of cake mix over cherries in each cup. Place dot of margarine on top. Bake at 350°F. thirty minutes, until golden brown. Run knife around edge and invert onto serving plate or serve right in dessert cups. *Serves 6-8.*

Cherry-Vanilla Pie

1 package instant vanilla pudding	2 cups pitted cherries
Pie Shell (baked or graham cracker)	

Prepare instant pudding mix. Pour into pie shell. Let stand five minutes to partially set. Refrigerate while setting. Arrange cherries over pudding. Chill one hour. *Serves 6.*

Cherry Cheese Whip

1 pound cottage cheese	2 tablespoons milk
1 teaspoon lemon extract	1 cup pitted cherries

Whip cottage cheese, extract and milk in blender until smooth. Add a bit more milk if necessary. Spoon into fancy sherbet or dessert dishes. Spoon fresh cherries over top. Refrigerate until ready to serve. *Serves 6-8.*

Cherry Drop Cookies

1 package cake mix (1 layer)	1 egg
4 tablespoons milk	1 cup pitted cherries
3 tablespoons margarine	

Mix all ingredients except cherries. Stir thoroughly until smooth. Drop by teaspoonfuls onto greased (or Teflon) cookie sheet. Press one cherry gently into center of cookie. Bake at 375°F. ten to twelve minutes. *Makes about two dozen cookies.*

Cherry Cream

1 cup pitted cherries	1 tablespoon lemon juice
1/2 cup sugar	1 cup sour cream

Combine cherries, sugar and lemon juice in saucepan. Cook until soft, about twenty minutes. Cool in refrigerator two hours. Combine with sour cream. Pour into individual dessert dishes. Place in freezer about one hour. Remove from freezer ten minutes before serving. *Serves 5-6.*

GRAPES

Peanut Butter-Grape Tarts

2 cups seedless grapes (Concord and Caco Good)	3/4 cup chunky peanut butter
	6 baked tart shells

In a double boiler combine and heat grapes and peanut butter. Cook gently about fifteen minutes until smooth and well mixed. Spoon into tart shells. Let stand to set and cool. Serve at room temperature with small scoop of vanilla ice cream on top. Don't blame us for this one—invented and adored by the children.

Grape Salad

1 cup diced cucumber (about 1
   medium)
1/2 green pepper, diced
2 tablespoons chopped fresh
   chives

2 cups green seedless grapes
Lettuce

Combine cucumber, pepper, chives and grapes. Toss gently. Arrange on individual plates on a bed of lettuce. Spoon 1 tablespoon favorite dressing over top. *Serves 6.*

MELON

Melon Dessert

1 cantaloupe
1 honeydew

1 cup blueberries
1 cup red raspberries

Cut melons in half. Remove juice and pits. Use melon baller to remove flesh from all four halves. Combine all fruits in large bowl. Be sure outer skins of melons are thoroughly scrubbed and look nice. Spoon mixture into one-half of honeydew and one-half of cantaloupe. Set one at each end of table. Spoon into dessert or sherbet dishes. Sprinkle with coconut. Serve with fancy cookies, coffee or tea. Marvelous afternoon treat for the ladies. *Serves 4.*

Melon Luncheon Salad

3 cantaloupes
1 cup seedless grapes

1 cup strawberries
1 cup peaches, diced

Cut melons in half. Remove juice and pits. Combine all other fruits. Spoon into cavity in melon. Keep chilled until ready to serve. Serve with hot bread or rolls, coffee and a light pastry for a superb and simple luncheon. *Serves 6.*

Melon Rings

Cut melon into thick rings. Remove seeds. Use hole in center to hold berries, grapes, cottage cheese, ice cream (with berries or jam, or apple butter over it), etc.

Party Centerpiece Dessert

1 watermelon
1 cantaloupe
1 honeydew

2 cups fresh peeled peach quarters
2 cups fresh peeled pear quarters

Cut watermelon in half horizontally with a zig-zag design. Carefully cut fruit out of one half (reserve second half for refills). Peel and cut other melons into bite-size chunks. Combine all melons and fruit in very large bowl. Spoon into watermelon shell. Place on large serving platter with large serving spoon. Use as centerpiece and allow to remain on table for dessert. *Serves 12 at least.*

PEACHES

Quick Peach Cobbler

1 eight-ounce package white or yellow layer cake mix
Peaches

1 tablespoon lemon juice
1 teaspoon cinnamon
1/4 cup sugar

Prepare cake mix as directed (or make your own favorite batter). Pour into greased and floured 8-inch-square baking pan. Carefully arrange sliced or halved peaches over top of batter. If halves are used, lay out the pattern so each serving can consist of one peach half on a nice square chunk of cake. Sprinkle lemon juice over peaches. Combine cinnamon and sugar. Sprinkle over top. Bake at 350°F. for about one hour (may even take a bit longer for peaches to cook and cake to turn golden brown). Fantastic served warm with sour cream or whipped cream. *Serves 9.*

Not So Quick Peach Cobbler

2 cups sliced peaches
1 cup sugar
4 tablespoons butter or margarine
1 egg

1/2 teaspoon vanilla extract
1 cup sifted flour
1/4 teaspoon salt
1 teaspoon baking powder
1/4 cup milk

Mix peaches and one-half cup sugar. Grease bottom of 9-inch-square baking dish. Line dish with fruit. Cream shortening and sugar. Add egg. Mix well. Add vanilla. Sift together flour, salt and baking powder. Add alternately with milk. Stir well. Pour batter over fruit. Bake at 400°F. for twenty-five to thirty minutes. *Serves 9.*

Spiced Peaches

1 pint fresh or preserved
   peaches
1/4 cup vinegar
1/2 cup sugar
12 whole cloves

1/8 teaspoon cinnamon
1 three-ounce package orange
   gelatin
3/4 cup cold water

Drain and chop peaches. Reserve three-quarters cup syrup. (If fresh peaches are used merely use another three-quarters cup water to make up for the syrup.) Combine and bring to a boil: vinegar, sugar and spices. Add peaches. Simmer ten minutes. Strain syrup and discard cloves. Add boiling water, if necessary, so you have one cup. Dissolve gelatin in hot syrup. Add cold water and peaches. Pour into individual molds or single small mold. Chill several hours until firm (overnight is better). *Serves 6.*

Chewy Peach Delight

2 cups peeled and sliced
   peaches
1 tablespoon lemon juice
1/2 teaspoon cinnamon
1 tablespoon butter or margarine
3 tablespoons brown sugar

6 tablespoons flour
1/8 teaspoon salt
1/3 cup rolled oats or crisp
   cereal flakes
3 tablespoons melted butter or
   margarine

Arrange peaches in greased shallow baking pan and sprinkle with lemon juice and cinnamon. Dot with butter. Combine remaining ingredients and mix until crumbly. Spread over peaches. Bake at 375°F. about thirty minutes. Serve with whipped cream or ice cream. *Serves 4-6.*

Peach Fritters

3/4 cup flour
1 tablespoon sugar
1/8 teaspoon salt
1 tablespoon liquid vegetable
   oil

1 egg, well-beaten
6 ripe fresh peaches (or preserved)
Nutmeg

Sift together flour, sugar and salt. Add oil and egg. Chop peaches. Stir into batter. Drop by large spoonfuls onto hot, greased griddle (or deep-fat fry, until golden brown), fry one side, then turn and brown other side. Drain on paper toweling. Serve sprinkled with a dash of nutmeg. *Serves 6-8.*

Crunchy Peach Dessert

1 quart preserved peaches
1/2 cup raisins
1/2 cup chopped walnuts
2 cups graham cracker crumbs

4 tablespoons melted butter or
   margarine
2 tablespoons lemon juice
1/2 cup brown sugar

Drain peaches. Chop. Combine all other ingredients. Mix thoroughly. Fold in peaches. Grease a shallow 9- x 13- x 2-inch baking pan. Pour in peach mixture. Bake at 350°F. about thirty minutes. Watch last five minutes. If getting too brown, remove. *Serves 12.*

Quick and Easy Peach Desserts

1) Fill peach halves with sour or whipped cream, sprinkle with brown sugar, add a touch of cinnamon if desired. Brown under broiler if desired or serve cold.

2) Top one-inch cake slices, or tart or meringue shell with a peach half. Bake at 425°F. Fill with ice cream. Serve with fresh or frozen raspberries.

3) Arrange peach halves in a baked pie shell. Melt red currant jelly, spread over peaches. Chill.

4) Fill peach halves with grapes and/or other fruit. Serve with a sweetened fruit dressing.

5) Fill peach halves with orange or lemon sherbet. Sprinkle with fresh blueberries. Pour ginger ale over all.

6) Arrange fruit, hollow side up, in a shallow baking dish. Combine one-half cup boiling water, one-quarter cup sugar and two teaspoons lemon juice. Pour over fruit and sprinkle with two tablespoons brown sugar. Bake about thirty minutes, until tender.

Company Peach Crisp

14 cups sliced peaches	3 3/4 cups rolled oats *15/4 C*
2 1/2 cups packed brown sugar *5/2 C*	1 tablespoon and 1 1/2 teaspoons cinnamon *10 t + 1/2 t*
1 tablespoon salt *9 t*	1 1/2 teaspoons nutmeg *3/2 t*
2 1/4 cups sifted cake flour *9/4 C*	1 2/3 cups shortening *5/3 C*

Drain peaches and set aside. Blend together brown sugar and salt. Add flour, rolled oats, cinnamon and nutmeg and mix well. Add shortening to dry ingredients; work in to form a crumbly mixture. Lightly grease two 9- x 13-inch baking pans. Sprinkle and lightly press crumb mixture into each pan. Do not use all crumb mixture. Cover each pan with sliced peaches, top with remaining crumb mixture. Bake at 375°F. approximately twenty-five minutes or until crust is crisp. *Yield: 25 portions.*

PEARS

Cinnamon Pears

3-4 ripe pears	2 teaspoons cinnamon
1/2 cup sugar	1/2 cup raisins
1 cup water	1/2 cup chopped walnuts

Peel and quarter pears. Remove core. Mix sugar, water and cinnamon until sugar and cinnamon dissolve. Add six drops red food coloring if you wish to turn everything a lovely rosy pink. Add fruit gently and simmer until tender but not mushy. Add raisins and nuts—cook five more minutes. Serve warm or cold. For variety, try green food coloring instead and use about 1/2 capful of peppermint extract in place of the cinnamon. *Serves 3-4.*

Fresh Pears Baked in Grenadine

3 firm pears	Juice of 1/2 lemon
1 cup grenadine	

Preheat oven to 325 °F. Peel pears. Cut in half lengthwise and remove core. Place, cut side down, in baking pan. Combine grenadine and lemon juice. Pour over pears and bake forty-five to fifty minutes. Baste frequently with syrup. Chill. *Serves 6.* Apples can be used instead of pears.

Pear Pie Plus

2 unbaked pie crusts	6 tablespoons brown sugar
3 cups sliced pears	Pinch salt
3 cups sliced peaches (or ap-	4 tablespoons flour
ples or blueberries)	1/2 teaspoon nutmeg
2 tablespoons lemon juice	3 tablespoons butter
1/2 cup sugar	

Place one unbaked pie crust in pie pan. Combine fruits with lemon juice. Toss gently to mix. Combine sugars, salt, flour and nutmeg. Pour over fruit and toss lightly to mix. Pour into pie shell. Dot with butter. Cover with second crust. Seal edges and trim. Cut slits in top. Bake forty-five minutes until top crust is golden brown. *Serves 8.*

Minted Pear Luncheon Mold

4 fresh pears	1/4 teaspoon mint extract
1 package lime gelatin	

Peel pears and cut in half. Prepare gelatin. Add mint to gelatin. Divide into four dessert dishes. Place pears in gelatin. Allow to set for about three hours. Unmold onto bed of lettuce. Serve with a ball of cottage cheese or pour three tablespoons of plain yogurt or sour cream over top. *Serves 4.*

PLUMS

Plum Mold

1 package lemon gelatin
2 cups halved and pitted
   fresh plums

1 cup cold orange juice

Prepare gelatin with three-quarter cup boiling water and one cup orange juice. Chill until it begins to set. Fold in plum halves. Chill until set in loaf pan. Serve slices plain or over slice of pound cake. *Serves 6-8.*

Plum Sauce

1 quart fresh plums, pitted
3/4 cup sugar

1 tablespoon lemon juice

Combine all ingredients in blender. Puree until smooth. Chill and serve over vanilla ice cream, pound cake, pound cake and vanilla ice cream, peach halves, melon balls, pancakes or anything else that appeals to you. *Makes about 2 1/2 cups.*

STRAWBERRIES

Fresh Strawberry Cheese Pie

4 cups fresh strawberries
1 8-ounce package cream
   cheese
1 pint heavy cream, whipped

1 baked 9" pie shell (or individual tart shells)
1 cup sugar

Wash, hull and drain berries. Set aside to drain thoroughly. Soften cream cheese and mix with whipped cream. Pour into pie shell and spread evenly. Select choice, perfect berries and arrange in pie shell. Press very gently into cheese. Mash rest of berries. Put into saucepan with sugar. Stir and cook about fifteen minutes or until mixture begins to feel slightly thickened. Cool. Pour over berries and cheese in pie shell. Refrigerate several hours before serving. Serve each slice with a dollop of whipped cream and one perfect berry on top. Gorgeous, quick and easy. *Serves 8-10.*

Strawberry Pancakes

Packaged or favorite pancake
mix

1 cup slightly mashed fresh
strawberries

Prepare pancake batter. Add strawberries. Make pancakes. Serve with strawberry syrup.

Quick Strawberry Pie

1 graham cracker crust or 1
9" baked pie crust

1 package vanilla pudding
2 cups fresh strawberries

Prepare vanilla pudding. Pour into pie shell. Slice berries in half and arrange, cut side down, over pudding. Chill several hours. *Serves 8-10.*

SOME SPECIAL SUGGESTIONS

Fruit Suggestions

1) Apple Dumplings also Peach Dumplings.
2) Apple Brown Betty or Peach Brown Betty.
3) Dessert pancakes, or crepes, filled with fruit, rolled up and sprinkled with sugar.
4) Apple pancakes (peach, blueberry). To pancake batter, add chopped fruit or berries. Make several small pancakes or one very large one. (Don't make it so big you can't turn it.) Or sprinkle with sugar and cinnamon and bake about ten minutes, until baked through.
5) Use apple, peach or pear chunks on top of a mound of cottage cheese. Sprinkle with sugar and cinnamon or raisins and chopped nuts for a quick and delicious lunch.

Miriam's Pie Crust

2 cups flour	2/3 cup solid shortening
2 tablespoons sugar	1/4 cup water
1/2 teaspoon salt	

Mix all dry ingredients. Then add shortening and mix well (using your hands only). Add water and continue mixing with hands. If too dry add more water, a tiny bit at a time until dough holds together. Refrigerate, wrapped in waxed paper, fifteen minutes.

Divide in two balls. Place each ball between two sheets of waxed paper. Roll out dough until right size for pie pan. Peel off top sheet of paper and put it back on. Turn it over. Peel off second piece. Turn back again and place in pie pan. Remove remaining waxed paper. Fill pie shell as desired. Repeat same method for top crust. Seal edges by pressing with the tines of a fork. Trim edges with sharp knife. Perforate with fork. Bake according to directions given for particular pie. *Yield: 2 9-inch crusts.*

Molded Gelatin Fruit Desserts

Flavored gelatin	2 cups fresh fruit (in any combination except pineapple)

Prepare gelatin. If you are fussy about whether or not fruit falls to bottom, refrigerate until gelatin begins to thicken. Then fold fruit in, it will stay where you put it. If you are not fussy, just add the fruit immediately, it will probably fall to the bottom. Put into bowl or mold or dessert dishes or eight-inch cake pan. Refrigerate several hours until set. Serve as is or with cookies on the side or coconut or chopped nuts sprinkled over top. If you wish, you may also put gelatin into loaf pan. Serve slices of gelatin over slices of pound cake or vanilla ice cream.

CHAPTER 6

Preserving
For Everyone

EVERYBODY'S DOING IT. Suddenly it has become the "in" thing. It's fun, it's productive, it's economical and it's healthier.

This new "thing" is the current revived enthusiasm in home canning, home jam and jelly making and home preserving of all kinds. Seems as if everyone is doing it and no one is in a better position than you. Imagine the delight of being able to enjoy premier taste and quality all year round. Can you begin to imagine the pride and sense of accomplishment you'll get from putting up your own garden fresh fruits and vegetables?

Time was when canning meant hours and hours over a hot stove and baskets and baskets of produce all over the kitchen. Though it would be nice to have basketsful of beautiful fruits and vegetables to preserve, today's canning and preserving are done in batches as small as a single half-pint. As a matter of fact, it's a lot more fun to can a few jars at a time than it is to spend a full day and night up to your elbows in produce, pots, pans and processing. Besides, few things that grow in the garden become ripe at the same time so stagger your canning a bit and enjoy it a lot more.

Almost everything that grows in your garden can be preserved by canning—a term that means preserving food by heating and sealing in airtight containers—in jars as well as cans. The term includes preserving fruits and vegetables (we're only interested in these two items, but meat, poultry, fish, soups and sauces can also be canned) just as they come from the garden, and in various other forms and combinations such as jams, jellies, preserves, conserves, pickles and relishes. And, done according to instructions, canning of every type can be safe, simple and genuinely pleasurable.

Several ground rules must be followed to the letter if you are to get the best results from your equipment (we use so few "things" they really shouldn't be called equipment) and from your produce.

First, use only perfect fruits and vegetables when you preserve. You may eat spotted or blemished produce, but do not use them in preserving. Anything less than perfect can encourage spoilage and that's the last thing you want. Similarly, use only perfect equipment. If you use a steam-pressure canner, check and clean petcock (vent) and safety valve openings. Check the pressure gauge on your canner to see that it is giving accurate readings. If you are going to use a water-bath canner see that it is not rusted, that the cover fits tight and the inner wire or wooden rack is in good shape.

Check out the containers you are going to use. See that there are no chips, cracks, dents or rust on cans, jar caps or gaskets. Make sure you have enough of everything you need by checking the manufacturer's list and replacing anything where conditions are in any way doubtful.

Examine carefully the manufacturer's instructions for the proper method for filling and sealing containers. Do not ad lib. Cook and process each item exactly as recommended and for the exact amount of time suggested for the specific kind of food being canned. Do not get involved in any fad, "quick" or "trick" processing methods. There are no safe shortcuts in canning or preserving. Follow instructions and you will have delicious canned and preserved fruits and vegetables. Do the job your own way or some "extra special time-saving way" and you may end up with spoiled food or your entire family being ill. Play it safe and accurate, and success and good taste will be your reward.

It is important here to include a warning about botulism. It is possible (but far from probable) for this deadly poison to be present in canned non-acid vegetables if the proper canning procedures were not followed. If the processing time recommended by the processing equipment manufacturer is followed, and all equipment is in good working order, there is no danger of botulism poisoning. However, to insure against even the remotest of possibilities, it is recommended that all low-acid foods canned at home be boiled for fifteen minutes before serving or *even tasting.* This extra precaution will either indicate the spoilage (it becomes much more apparent when heat is applied) or will eliminate all danger since boiling for fifteen minutes destroys this microorganism, making the food absolutely safe to eat.

There are three different methods of canning, one for each different kind of food to be processed. That is, the kind of food determines the processing method which, in turn, determines the kind of equipment you will need.

Low-acid vegetables, including asparagus, all kinds of beans, beets, broccoli, Brussels sprouts, cabbage, carrots, cauliflower, celery, corn, eggplant, peas, peppers, potatoes (white and sweet), pumpkin, spinach and all its green relatives and most members of the squash family, must be processed at a temperature of 240° F. This method uses a steam-pressure canner, also called a pressure cooker, to supply enough heat to destroy all types of spoilage bacteria. The cooker is a heavy kettle equipped with a cover that can be clamped or locked onto the kettle making it steam tight. The top of the canner comes with a gauge, a safety valve and a vent.

Though each low-acid vegetable has a specific cooking time and recipe for canning, the following instructions for canning green beans may be considered to be fairly typical. For additional recipes and exact canning times, check the booklets that are supplied by the manufacturers of your pressure cooker or by the manufacturer of the jars or cans you will use.

Start each canning session by getting everything you need set and ready for action. Read all about the vegetables to be canned in the manufacturer's instruction book. Check, clean and arrange everything you will need on or near your work area. This includes jars and cans (make sure they're perfect), pressure cooker (especially check out valves, vents and gauges), and, most important of all, the vegetables. Use only the best and freshest (two hours from garden to canner is excellent) and then wash, drain, trim, cut or break, in that order according to recipe. Wash jars in hot soapy water, rinse and keep standing in hot water until you use them.

Working as quickly as possible, prepare enough vegetables to fill a single canner load. Always work in single canner load batches so there are no leftovers or waste. Place prepared vegetables in a large pot with boiling water and boil for five minutes. Many vegetables can be packed raw so you may want to skip this step. If you do cook the vegetables you may want to add about one teaspoon of salt for each quart. Pack the vegetables into the jars just loosely enough for water to circulate through the jar but do not waste space. Cover the vegetables with the boiling water in which they were cooked and leave a one-inch headspace. Remove all air bubbles from the jar by running a rubber scraper carefully around the jar.

With a clean, damp cloth wipe off the jar top and threads. Cap as described by manufacturer of brand you are using. Place the completed jars into the canner's rack. Add two or three inches of boiling water according to manufacturer's directions. Put the canner cover on and lock into place. Place pot over heat and allow steam to escape through the vent for ten minutes. Close the vent and bring the pressure to ten pounds. This is the point at which you start counting processing time. If you live at an altitude of 2,000 feet or more, you must process at the following pressures:

Altitude	Process at pressures of:
2,000— 3,000 feet	11 1/2 pounds
3,000— 4,000 feet	12 pounds
4,000— 5,000 feet	12 1/2 pounds
5,000— 6,000 feet	13 pounds
6,000— 7,000 feet	13 1/2 pounds
7,000— 8,000 feet	14 pounds
8,000— 9,000 feet	14 1/2 pounds
9,000—10,000 feet	15 pounds

Process for as long as recommended by the manufacturer, then remove the canner from the heat and wait while the pressure falls to zero. Wait an additional two minutes after the gauge is at zero before slowly opening the vent. Remove the cover by tipping it away from you so steam comes out away from you.

Carefully remove jars and stand them on a towel-padded counter or wood surface to cool. Space the jars about three or four

Wash, trim and cut or break perfect beans.

Cover with boiling water and boil for five minutes.

Add salt, pack and cover with boiling water—leave headspace.

Wipe jar top, put lid on and screw band on jar.

Put jars into steam-pressure canner containing hot water.

Lock cover. Place canner over heat.

Let steam escape from vent for ten minutes. Close vent.

Allow jars to cool. Keep them separated from each other. Check for seal.

inches each away from the other jars, and allow to cool, slowly, out of drafts for about twelve hours. Then, check the caps for seal. If any haven't sealed you can either repack and reprocess or put them into the refrigerator and use as quickly as possible. Remove jar bands (when using two-piece tops) and store the jars in a dry, dark, reasonably cool spot. Then, the next time you want the best vegetables anywhere, go to your storage spot, take a jar or two, cook and enjoy.

There is no really accurate rule of thumb to use in determining the number of jars of vegetables you can get from a given amount of fresh vegetables. It depends on vegetable variety, maturity, size of pieces, the way they are packed and other considerations. The following chart will give you an approximation of the amounts of fresh vegetables required to make one quart of canned vegetables:

Asparagus	4 lbs.
Lima Beans	4 lbs.
Green Beans	2 1/2 lbs.
Beets	3 lbs.
Carrots	3 lbs.
Corn	5 lbs.
Peas	5 lbs.
Pumpkin	3 lbs.
Spinach	5 lbs.
Squash	4 lbs.
Sweet Potatoes	3 lbs.

The second canning method is called the water-bath method and it is used for processing fruits and acid vegetables. In this category are such things as apples, berries, cherries, grapes, peaches, pears, plums and the acid vegetables rhubarb, tomatoes and sour cabbage. For this method all you need is a very large pot or kettle that has a cover and a rack or metal basket to keep the jars off the bottom of the pot. The pot must be deep enough to accommodate quart jars with two inches of water covering their tops.

As an example, we will use the instructions for canning peaches, but suggest you check your manufacturer's instruction book for times and recipes for other specific fruits and acid vegetables. All the preparatory instructions for canning peaches are identical to those indicated for green beans. To peel the peaches, put several into a wire basket and set the basket into boiling water. Let the peaches sit in the boiling water for about one minute, dunk into ice water and quickly peel off the skin.

Cut the peeled peaches in half and remove the pit. Slip the peach halves into a solution of two tablespoons vinegar in a gallon of cold water to prevent discoloration. When you're set to put the peaches into the jars, rinse fruit in cold water to remove any trace of vinegar. Pack the peaches into the jars, pit side down in overlapping layers. Cover the peaches with boiling hot syrup leaving only 1/2-inch headspace. You can figure on using about 1 1/2 cups of syrup for each quart jar. To make light syrup mix, heat two cups of sugar to a quart of water (5 cup yield); medium syrup, three cups sugar to a quart of water (5 1/2 cup yield); and for heavy syrup, 5 cups sugar to one quart of water (6 1/2 cup yield).

Remove air bubbles, wipe jar tops and threads, screw on caps and place each jar, as it is filled, into the rack sitting in three inches of hot water in the canner bottom. Add jars until the canner (pot or kettle) is full; then add more water until it covers jars with at least 1 1/2 to 2 inches of water. Bring water to a boil and process quarts for thirty minutes at a gentle, steady boil. If you live at an altitude of 1,000 feet or more you must add to your water bath processing as follows:

	Increase in processing time if the time called for is:	
Altitude	**20 minutes or less**	**more than 20 minutes**
1,000 feet.	1 minute	2 minutes
2,000 feet.	2 minutes	4 minutes
3,000 feet.	3 minutes	6 minutes
4,000 feet.	4 minutes	8 minutes
5,000 feet.	5 minutes	10 minutes
6,000 feet.	6 minutes	12 minutes
7,000 feet.	7 minutes	14 minutes
8,000 feet.	8 minutes	16 minutes
9,000 feet.	9 minutes	18 minutes
10,000 feet.	10 minutes	20 minutes

Wash and rinse nondefective jars and lids. Leave in hot water.

Sort, wash and drain enough peaches for single load.

Dip peaches in boiling water to loosen skin.

Halve, pit and peel. Drop into salt-vinegar water. Rinse.

Pack in overlapping design
into hot jar.
Add boiling syrup.

Remove all air bubbles.
Add more syrup.
Leave headspace. Cap.

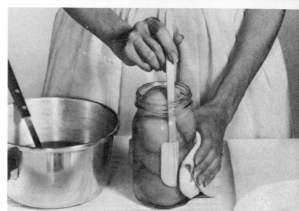

Put filled jars into canner
containing hot water.

Cover. Bring to boil.
Process at a gentle,
steady boil.

As mentioned previously, there is no more accurate measure for yield of fruit and acid vegetables than there is for low-acid vegetables. The following chart gives an approximation of the amounts needed to make one quart of canned produce:

Apples	3 lbs.
. Applesauce	3 1/2 lbs.
Berries	3 lbs.
Cherries	2 1/2 lbs.
Peaches	3 lbs.
Pears	3 lbs.
Plums	3 lbs.
Tomatoes	3 1/2 lbs.

The third canning method is called the open-kettle method and it is only used for jams, jellies, conserves, preserves, relishes and some pickles. In this method, the food is cooked in an uncovered kettle or pot and then poured directly, boiling hot, into sterilized hot jars. Each jar is sealed immediately after filling and before any others are filled. No further processing is required.

JAMS

All of these fruit products are pretty much alike since all are made of fruit preserved by sugar and jelled somewhat. The differences come from the kinds of fruit used, the way they are used, the amounts of various ingredients and their proportions and the method and length of cooking. Jam is made from fruit that has been ground or crushed. It holds its shape, but not nearly as well as jelly does. Jelly is made from fruit juice; it is clear and firm enough so that it holds its shape when turned out of a jar or cup. Conserves are really jams made with two or more kinds of fruit, often with the addition of raisins and nuts. Preserves are whole fruits or very large pieces of fruit in a very thick syrup which is sometimes jelled a bit.

The basic jam-making method has many variations and proportions, but all rely on the following:

Combine freshly picked fruit with sugar and slowly bring to a boil. The proportion of fruit and sugar depends upon the particular fruit, how ripe it is and your personal preference. Some recipes call for lemon juice and this should be added at the outset. Bring the mixture to a boil very slowly. Stir so sugar melts and then mixes with and dissolves into the fruit.

When sugar is completely dissolved, cook the mixture at a rapid boil for twenty to thirty minutes. Be sure the pot you use is large enough to allow for a high boil. Stir frequently to prevent sticking or scorching. Continue to cook until mixture starts to thicken (if you are using a candy or jelly thermometer remove the pot from heat just as soon as pointer reaches the jelly mark). Pour the thickened jam immediately into sterilized jars and seal according to manufacturer's directions.

The basic recipes that follow will give you an idea of the proportions that are suggested for the most popular jams. All fruits should be washed in cold water and drained. Wash several times, if necessary, but never let fruit stand in water.

Apple Jam

4 cups peeled, cored, chopped   4 cups sugar
    apples

(As with apple butter, 2 teaspoons ground cinnamon and 1/4 teaspoon ground cloves may be added if desired.)

Berry Jams

Blackberry, blueberry, boysenberry, dewberry, gooseberry, loganberry, raspberry, youngberry

3 cups crushed berries   2 cups sugar

These proportions make exactly 2 one-half pint jars. (7 cups fruit and 4 2/3 cups sugar yield 2 pints and 2 one-half pint jars.) Depending on the amount of fruit you have, the proportion of berries to sugar is: 1 cup fruit to 2/3 cup sugar.

Bring fruit-sugar combination to boil until it starts to thicken.

Check thickness by "sheeting" or use jelly thermometer.

Pour boiling hot into sterilized jars.

Seal jars according to manufacturer's directions.

Turn upside down for 10 seconds so boiling liquid covers jar top.

Cherry Jam

1 cup fresh sweet pitted   2/3 cup sugar
   cherries

Use these proportions for as many cups of cherries as you have. Don't make more than six cups of fruit at one time. Makes approximately 1/2 pint jam for each 1 1/4 cups fruit used.

Grape Jam

7 cups grapes   5 1/2 cups sugar

Put through food blender or chopper. Cook about fifteen minutes. Put through food mill to remove pits. Return to pot, add sugar and cook as usual. Makes approximately 5 one-half-pint jars.

Peach Jam

8 cups peeled crushed peaches   6 cups sugar

(1 teaspoon whole cloves, 1/2 teaspoon allspice plus 1 stick cinnamon may be placed in a cheesecloth bag while jam is boiling if you wish a spiced jam. Be sure to remove bag before filling jars.) Makes approximately 9 one-half-pint jars.

Pear Jam

4 cups peeled, cored and   3 1/2 cups sugar (or 2 1/2
   chopped pears   cups sugar and 1 cup hon-
                                      ey)
                                   1 tablespoon lemon juice

Makes approximately 5 one-half-pint jars.

Plum Jam

2 quarts pitted chopped plums   1/3 cup lemon juice
5-6 cups sugar   Boiling water

This takes a bit of experimenting to achieve personal satisfaction. A bit more or less sugar or lemon juice may be needed to please you. Also, keep some water on the boil while boiling the jam in case it thickens too rapidly.

Strawberry Jam

5 cups strawberries   1/3 cup lemon juice (optional)
4 1/2 cups sugar

If lemon juice is added, jam will be a lighter, truer strawberry color. Also, depending upon personal preference, many feel it enhances the flavor. Makes about 4-5 one-half-pint jars.

JELLY

Jelly-making is a bit different, requiring a jelly bag to get the juice from the ripe fruit. This bag, available at most department or hardware stores, holds the fruit and allows the juice to drain out. The clearest jelly comes from juice that has drained through a jelly bag with no squeezing. You get a lot more juice from your fruit if you do some squeezing. If you must squeeze, re-strain the juice through double-thick, damp cheesecloth before using to make jelly.

To prepare juice, clean and crush about three quarts of berries. Use one-quarter under-ripe fruit to every three-quarters ripe fruit so no artificial pectin need be added. Under-ripe fruit has a higher natural pectin content than fully ripe fruit so the one-to-three proportion balances nicely. Add one cup of water to the juice. Cover and rapidly bring to a boil. Lower heat and continue cooking very gently for about seven minutes. Put the cooked berries into a damp jelly bag. Let the berries drip by themselves (only squeeze if you're in a big hurry—which isn't the way to make jelly). Make sure you have five cups of juice and combine them with the sugar. Boil the juice and sugar rapidly, stirring frequently to prevent sticking or scorching. Continue to cook the mixture until it reaches 8 °F. above the boiling point of water. To determine boiling point in your area, boil water and take reading on candy thermometer.

Remove from heat, quickly skim off any foam which appears on the top of the jelly, pour into hot sterilized jars and seal according to manufacturer's directions. Makes about 5 half-pint jars.

Damp jelly bag holds cooked berries and allows their juice to drip into bowl. Add sugar to juice, boil and you've got unbelievable jelly.

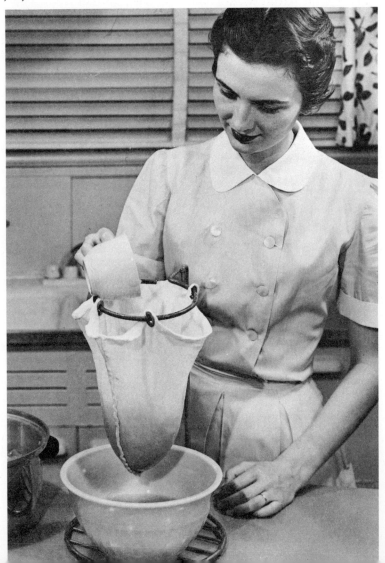

Often the biggest problem is trying to figure out when the jelly is done. Using a jelly or candy thermometer should just about eliminate the problem. Check your thermometer against the temperature of rapidly boiling water. If you cook your jelly to 8°F. higher than the temperature of the boiling water you should get consistently good results.

When making jelly without the addition of pectin, the result is sometimes a jelly that is too firm. In this case, shorten the cooking time. If the jelly is too soft, cook it just a bit more.

A typical recipe would call for five cups of blackberry juice to each three and one-half cups of sugar. Consider also apple, cherry, crabapple, grape, strawberry and plum jelly. All are made the same way and come out tasting fruity and delicious.

You may also combine various juices, in various proportions to make interesting and uniquely flavorful jellies. Experiment and you will find taste treats you never dreamed existed, and combinations to please and delight each member of the family. It's also a wonderful way to utilize small amounts of various juices. You may even freeze these juices separately, until you have enough to combine and make into jelly. You might even prepare several kinds of juices, can or freeze them (unsweetened) at the peak of the season, put them away and make the jelly later on at your convenience.

CONSERVES

Conserves are very much like jam in preparation and consistency, but are made by combining several different kinds of fruit. In addition, a true conserve should combine the fruits and sugar with raisins and nuts.

The basic method for preparing conserves is exactly the same as for jam. If nuts are included, they should be added during the last five minutes of cooking.

The conserve offers the opportunity for combining different fruit flavors as well as types. It is also a wonderful way to use small amounts of various ingredients allowing full use of all fruits, resulting in little waste if any.

Blueberry-Raspberry Conserve

3 cups blueberries

3 cups raspberries

1/2 cup seedless raisins

5 cups sugar

1/2 cup chopped walnuts

Combine berries, raisins and sugar. Slowly bring to a boil and stir occasionally. Once sugar dissolves, cook rapidly until mixture begins to thicken. Add nuts and cook an additional five minutes. Pour, boiling hot, into sterilized jars. Process according to manufacturer's directions.

Makes approximately 2 pints.

Consider such combinations as:

apple—peach

blueberry—pineapple

apple—cherry

blueberry—apple

raspberry—apple

blackberry—peach

Add such things as raisins, nuts, coconut, thinly sliced orange, lemon or lime (peel and all).

PRESERVES

Preserves are made with whole fruits, or large pieces, and sugar. They are prepared so the fruit retains its shape. Select only fruit that is firm-ripe. There are two basic methods for making preserves.

Strawberry Preserves No. 1

6 cups strawberries

5 cups sugar

Alternate layers of sugar and berries in a large pot and refrigerate overnight. Heat mixture to boiling and stir occasionally. Stir very gently so as not to crush or mash fruit. Boil rapidly, stirring often to prevent sticking or scorching, yet carefully so as not to damage the fruit. Cook until you reach a temperature of 9°F. above the boiling point of water (which usually takes about fifteen to twenty minutes). Remove from heat. Pour into sterilized jars and seal. Makes about 4 one-half-pint jars.

Strawberry Preserves No. 2

6 cups strawberries   1/4 cup lemon juice
5 cups sugar

Combine berries and sugar. Let stand for four hours. Bring slowly to a boil, stirring occasionally, until sugar dissolves. Add lemon juice. Cook rapidly about twelve to fifteen minutes until syrup begins to thicken and berries are clear. Pour into a shallow pan and let stand, uncovered, up to twenty-four hours. Make sure you keep them in a cool place, shaking them about once an hour (when awake) to keep berries evenly distributed in syrup. Pack into hot jars and process in a water-bath canner about twenty minutes (for both pints and half-pints) at 185°F. Makes about 4 one-half pints.

Consider apricot, cherry, peach, pear, plum, quince, strawberry, and combination preserves.

BUTTERS

Butters are thicker than jams and are cooked longer. They combine fruit pulp with sugar and are cooked very slowly once the sugar is added. If only 50% sugar to fruit pulp is used, the finished product should be processed ten minutes in a water-bath canner.

Apple Butter

Clean and quarter apples. Cook until soft. Put through food mill. Measure 1 cup sugar to 1 cup apple pulp. Cook slowly in heavy pot until sugar dissolves. Cook on low heat. Stir occasionally with a wooden spoon. Add 1 clove of ginger while cooking. Butters cook best when they are cooked slowest, so take your time. To test for doneness, take 1 teaspoonful—put it on a plate—wait one minute, if it doesn't run, it's ready. Jar and seal or freeze.

Consider making peach butters, spiced peach, pear or spiced pear, plum or apricot butters. Consider also the addition of some ginger, nutmeg, cinnamon, lemon or orange juice to enhance and bring out flavor of fruit.

CHAPTER 7

Freezing Fast
and Furious

To HEAR SOME people tell it, freezing is the "be all and end all" of food preservation. All you have to do is wrap something and stick it in the freezer. Then, some undetermined time in the future you take it out, heat it and, as if by magic, it is as fresh and tasty as it ever was. To a certain extent all this is true, but to a certain extent of course, it is grossly exaggerated.

For many foods freezing is the quickest, easiest home preservation method. Even more important than the simplicity and speed inherent in freezing is the convenience that comes from having a wide variety of foods ready in your home—when and how you want them. If you plan correctly you can always have an ample supply of your garden's bounty no matter the season or the weather.

As was the case with canning, freezing, too, has ground rules that must be followed if you are to get the best results. For example, it is important that you know that some varieties freeze better than others and you'd better know it beforehand if you are to avoid disappointment. Matter of fact, you should really know very far in advance, even before you plant the fruit or vegetable, so you can specify and buy only those plants which have fruit with superior freezing characteristics. Most of the varieties listed in earlier chapters are good varieties to plant if you expect to do

144

some freezing. To get the latest information, write to your agricultural college, state extension service or agricultural experiment station for the varieties that do best in your area and yield the highest quality when frozen.

Another important freezing rule goes something like, "You only get out what you put in." That is, if the quality of the fruits and vegetables is high before freezing, it will be high when you defrost and eat them. Use only the freshest, ripest produce for freezing. When you harvest fruits and vegetables for freezing, pick those that are "eating" ripe and freeze them immediately. The less time it takes the produce to go from garden to freezer the higher the quality will be.

It is also very important that the actual freezing takes place as quickly as possible. Put only the amount of unfrozen food into your home freezer that will freeze in twenty-four hours. To determine this: figure about three pounds of unfrozen food per cubic foot of freezer capacity will freeze solid in every twenty-four-hour period. For example, if you have a fourteen-cubic-foot freezer, freeze only about forty to forty-two pounds of unfrozen food at a time. To help this along as much as possible, never put hot foods into the freezer, and always pack and store food only after it has had sufficient time to cool off.

For best results when freezing foods, pack them in containers that are airtight, watertight, odorproof and vaporproof. Glass, metal and rigid plastic are examples of this type of container. Plastic bags, wrapping materials and waxed cartons made especially for freezing will also do a good job. Do not try to economize by using "regular" waxed paper or aluminum foil or reusing ice cream, milk or cottage cheese containers for freezing. These containers are not made for food freezing and the result will be that your fruits and vegetables will suffer considerable quality loss.

Because the whole idea behind packaging for freezing is to keep food from drying out, thus preserving food color, taste and nutritive value, it is especially important to eliminate as much air as possible from filled containers. Leave enough headspace to accommodate the food as it expands while freezing, but pack the remainder of the container as tightly as you can to eliminate as much air space as possible. Make sure sealing edges of containers are clean and that seals are completely airtight.

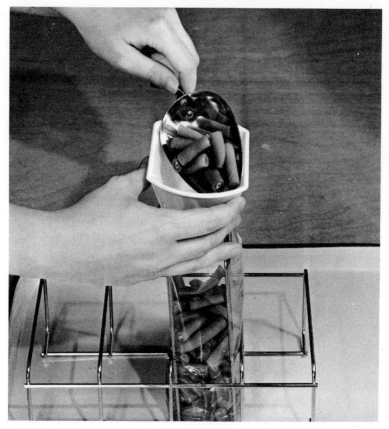

Plastic bags placed into cardboard boxes make fine freezing containers. Funnel helps keep sealing edges clean.

Remember, too, that fruits and vegetables have different storage periods; that is, the length of time the produce can be stored at 0°F. and still maintain very high quality, taste and texture. As a general rule, fruits and vegetables stay well in storage for eight to twelve months. After this, while still safe to eat, they start losing some of their taste and flavor and suffer some change in texture.

Freezing vegetables is quick and easy with only a few steps required. However, for best results, follow these steps carefully and do not substitute any shortcuts or other untested methods.

Directly from the garden, wash all vegetables thoroughly under cold water, but do not let them sit in water. (Allowing fruits and vegetables to sit in water can change their texture and

Blanch all vegetables (except peppers) by putting them into basket and lowering into boiling water. Blanch, do not cook vegetables.

drain them of taste and nutritive value.) Sort the vegetables according to size, color and degree of ripeness. Put aside those vegetables that are to be frozen whole. Peel, trim and cut the remainder according to the characteristics of the vegetables and your own preference.

The next step is the most important step of all when preparing vegetables for freezing. With the exception of green peppers, *all* vegetables must be blanched (also called scalded) before freezing. This heating process (the vegetables must be heated through) slows down or stops entirely the enzyme action that causes vegetables to discolor, lose their natural taste, take on off-flavors and become tough and totally unappetizing.

To blanch vegetables put them into a wire basket and lower it into boiling water. Complete blanchers (pot, basket and cover) are available at department and hardware stores, but you can improvise your own by combining these three parts from equipment you already have in your kitchen. Use at least one gallon of boiling water for each pound of vegetables in your blanching basket. As soon as the blanching basket is completely submerged in the boiling water, put the cover on the kettle and start timing. Correct times for home-grown vegetables are given along with other specific instructions later in this chapter.

As soon as the exact time has been reached for a particular vegetable (no more and no less), remove the blanching basket from the boiling water and plunge it into a sinkful of ice water. This will stop the vegetables from cooking any further and also cool them sufficiently to go right into the freezer. Allow the same amount of time for cooling as you did for cooking. When vegetables are cool, drain and pack them quickly into freezer containers. Seal containers and store as quickly as possible in freezer. Do not allow packages to stand around as you pack others— put them into coldest part of refrigerator as you prepare and pack remainder and then put all into freezer.

Use the following instructions for specific information on home-grown vegetables.

ASPARAGUS—Use only tenderest spears and compact tips. Wash and either cut into 1 1/2- to 2-inch pieces or leave whole and only cut if necessary to fit container. Blanch for two to four minutes, depending on thickness of stalks, or two minutes for cut pieces. Cool in ice water. Drain. Pack in containers. Leave *no* headspace. To get maximum efficiency from containers when packing asparagus spears whole, alternate first stalk, then tip end. Seal containers and freeze. 1 to 1 1/2 pounds of fresh asparagus yields 1 pint frozen.

LIMA BEANS—Shell and sort according to size. Use only young, green beans. Blanch in boiling water from two to four minutes according to size. Cool quickly and pack into containers. Leave one-half-inch headspace. Seal containers and freeze. 2 to 2 1/2 pounds of fresh limas will yield 1 pint frozen.

SNAP BEANS—Use only young beans that snap when broken (same for wax and green beans). Wash carefully in cold water and remove tips. Cut into style preferred by your family—sliced, kitchen-cut (diagonal), french (julienne) or leave whole. Blanch whole beans three minutes, sliced beans two minutes. Cool quickly in ice water, drain and pack into containers. Leave one-half-inch headspace. Seal containers and freeze. 1 pound of fresh beans yields 1 pint frozen.

BEETS—Use small, tender beets and remove tops and all but one-half-inch stems. Wash, sort according to size and cook as you would for serving fresh—about thirty minutes for small beets and forty-five minutes for larger ones. Cool quickly in cold water and slice as desired into discs, strings or cubes. Seal containers and freeze. 1 1/2 pounds of fresh beets yields 1 pint frozen.

BROCCOLI—Wash compact, dark green heads in cold water. Peel and trim stalks. Split into pieces so flowerets are about golf ball-size across. Blanch in boiling water for four minutes. Chill immediately. Pack into containers leaving no headspace. Seal containers and freeze. 1 pound of fresh broccoli yields 1 pint frozen.

Broccoli is packed into plastic containers so some flowerets are at each end. No headspace is required for this vegetable.

BRUSSELS SPROUTS—Select only young, green, compact heads. Trim off all tough outer leaves. Wash thoroughly. Sort according to size. Blanch small heads three minutes, medium heads four minutes and larger heads five minutes. Cool quickly and drain. Pack into containers leaving no headspace. Seal containers and freeze. 1 pound of fresh Brussels sprouts yields 1 pint frozen.

CABBAGE—Once frozen, cabbage can only be used as a cooked vegetable. Use solid, compact heads after tough outer leaves have been removed. Cut into small wedges or large shreds. Blanch in boiling water for one and one-half minutes. Cool, drain and pack into containers leaving one-half-inch headspace. Seal containers and freeze. 1 medium head of cabbage yields 2 pints frozen.

CARROTS—Pick slender, tender young carrots. Remove tops and tips, wash thoroughly and peel. Leave small carrots whole. Dice, slice or cut the bigger ones into shoestring style. Blanch small whole carrots five minutes and others two minutes. Cool immediately, drain and pack into containers leaving one-half-inch headspace. Seal containers and freeze. 1 1/2 pounds of fresh carrots yields 1 pint frozen.

CAULIFLOWER—Young, firm, light white heads are the best. Break head into flowerets and blanch in salt water (4 teaspoons salt per gallon of water) for three minutes. Cool quickly and drain. Pack into containers leaving no headspace. Seal containers and freeze. 2 medium heads of fresh cauliflower yields 3 pints frozen.

CORN—Use young ears for corn on the cob and whole-kernel-style. Use slightly older ears for cream-style corn. Husk, remove silk, wash and drain. Blanch corn on the cob seven minutes for small diameter ears (1 1/4 inches across) and eleven minutes for large diameter ears (over 1 1/2 inches across). Blanch other styles for four minutes. For whole kernel, cut kernels from cob at about two-thirds of their depth and for creamed style, about halfway through kernel (scrape cob with back of knife to get juice and kernel heart). Cool all corn quickly and drain. Pack off-cob corn into containers leaving one-half-inch headspace. Pack ears into containers leaving *no* headspace or wrap in special moisture-vapor resistant freezer material. Seal containers and freeze. 2 1/2 pounds of fresh corn yields 1 pint frozen.

EGGPLANT—Not a particularly good freezer, eggplant should be cut into manageable pieces and blanched. Add one tablespoon of lemon juice to each gallon of water used for blanching. Blanch eggplant for five minutes. Cool immediately and drain. Pack into containers leaving one-half-inch headspace. Seal containers and freeze. 1 medium-size eggplant yields 1 pint frozen.

GREENS—This group includes beet greens, chard, collards, kale, spinach and others. Use only tender, full-colored leaves. Wash thoroughly in cold running water. Remove tough stems and cut leaves or leave whole as desired. Blanch for two and one-half minutes. Cool immediately, drain and pack into containers leaving one-half-inch headspace. Seal containers and freeze. 1 1/2 pounds fresh greens yields 1 pint frozen.

PEPPERS—These can be frozen without blanching. Simply cut, remove stem and seeds and pack into containers leaving *no* headspace. If you are going to use peppers in cooking, cut, remove stem and seeds, cut into halves or pieces and blanch for two and one-half minutes. Cool and drain, then pack into containers leaving one-half-inch headspace. Seal containers and freeze. 3 fresh peppers yields 1 pint frozen.

PUMPKIN—Choose mature pumpkins and cut into manageable pieces. Remove all seeds and membranes. Cook until tender. Discard the rind after removing all pulp. Put the pulp through a sieve and mash. Cool by placing pan holding pulp into another pan filled halfway with ice water. Pack into containers leaving one-half-inch headspace. Seal containers and freeze. 3 pounds of fresh pumpkin yields 1 pint frozen.

SQUASH—Use same procedure as listed for pumpkin.

To cook frozen vegetables, simply break up the frozen mass (rap on a hard surface) and cook in about one-quarter cup of water to each pint package. Cook until tender but not soft. Frozen vegetables take considerably less time to cook than fresh vegetables because they have already been blanched in boiling water. Cook all vegetables, except corn on the cob, asparagus and the greens family, just as they come from the freezer. Corn must be fully thawed before cooking, and asparagus and greens should be partially thawed. Once cooked, prepare your frozen vegetables any way you like and enjoy the color, taste and flavor of garden fresh vegetables all year-round.

Freezing fruits is a considerably different story. Fruits are more perishable and many turn brown after cutting or peeling. Most should be packed in dry sugar or in syrup and few, if any, should be cooked before freezing. As a matter of fact, preparation of fruit to be frozen closely parallels preparation for serving fresh as a dessert or for use in cooking or baking.

All fruits except melons, peaches and pears can be packed and frozen in their natural state without either syrup or dry sugar. However, it should be noted that just about all fruits have better texture and flavor if packed in syrup. The suggestions that will follow shortly will call for packing in syrup, but the same directions can be followed for the freezing of these fruits without either syrup or dry sugar. If you prefer to pack fruit in dry sugar, simply add about three-quarters cup sugar, according to tartness, to each quart of fruit. Gently turn fruit over and over until sugar is absorbed and juices flow. Then follow same procedure as for syrup pack.

To make syrup, dissolve sugar in water and stir until all sugar disappears. Refrigerate and use cold when packing fruit. Most fruits are frozen in a medium syrup (40%), but some of the more tart fruits can be frozen in a heavier syrup. The proportions for syrups used in freezing fruits are:

Type of syrup	Sugar	Water	Yield of syrup
30 per cent	2 cups	4 cups	5 cups
40 per cent	3 cups	4 cups	5 1/2 cups
50 per cent	4 3/4 cups	4 cups	6 1/2 cups
60 per cent	7 cups	4 cups	7 3/4 cups

To keep all the fruit submerged in the syrup after filling a container and leaving headspace, crumple up a piece of parchment paper, place it on top of the fruit and press down. When you seal the container the closure will force the fruit down into the syrup. It is important to keep all the fruit deep down in the syrup or those pieces exposed to air in the headspace will change color and flavor during the time they are in storage.

Small piece of crumpled parchment paper is placed on top of fruit to keep them down in syrup and prevent color and flavor change.

All packages should be marked with name of fruit and date frozen. *Freeze solid and store at 0° F. or below.*

Since most fruits are usually packed in quart containers, the headspace requirements are given for wide-mouth quart containers. That is, leave one-inch headspace when packing fruits in syrup in these containers. If you should be packing in wide-mouth pint containers, allow one-half-inch headspace. Narrow-mouth containers are not really as easy to use and pack, but if you are using them, allow three-quarters of one-inch headspace when packing pints, and one and one-half inches when packing quarts. If you leave no headspace or too little headspace, the fruits and syrup will expand right out of your freezing container—usually ruining it and the fruit.

The following suggestions should give you an idea of what is required to freeze specific fruits in syrups. Remember that in almost all cases fruits can be very successfully canned, so you must make a decision on which preservation method best suits your needs, space and equipment situation. Check with the freezing materials manufacturer's booklets for any additional specific information.

APPLES—Frozen in 40% syrup this fruit can be used many, many different ways, but perhaps best in pies. Use only firm, crisp apples, not ones with a mealy texture. Wash, peel and core. Slice apples directly into container that holds the 40% syrup (figure 2 cups of syrup for each quart container). Fill the container leaving headspace. Push fruit down into syrup. Add syrup so all fruit is covered. Check headspace. Seal container and freeze. 1/2 bushel (about 25 pounds of fresh apples) will yield about 10 quarts frozen.

BERRIES—For freezing directions, this group of fruits must be broken into smaller subgroups. In the first are blackberries, boysenberries, dewberries, loganberries and youngberries. These can be frozen whole in the syrup pack. Select only fully ripe, firm berries. Sort, wash and drain. Berries that are either too young or too old may cause flavor changes. Pack berries into cold 40% or 50% syrup. (Can also be packed in dry sugar.) Leave headspace after all fruit is pushed down into syrup.

The second subgroup contains blueberries, elderberries and huckleberries. Choose only fully ripe berries about same size and color. Sort, wash and drain. Steam berries for no more than one minute and cool immediately. Pack cold into 40% syrup and leave headspace.

Gooseberries are best frozen unsweetened. Simply select the firmest fully ripe berries and pack them, after washing and draining into a container. Leave about one-half-inch headspace.

Grapes are best when frozen in syrup, but they can be packed without added sweetening if they are going to be used to make jelly or juice. Use only those grapes that are plump, ripe and fully colored. Wash and drain. Remove all stems. Seedless grapes should be left whole—table grapes should be split in half and the seeds removed. Pack into containers with 40% syrup. Leave headspace.

Raspberries can be frozen in any of the three ways. Use fully ripe, juicy berries. Sort, wash in cold water and drain. Pack in containers with 40% syrup. Leave headspace.

For sugar pack, add three-quarters-cup sugar to a quart (a bit over 1 pound) of berries. Turn berries over and over carefully until most of sugar is dissolved. Pack into containers leaving one-half-inch headspace.

All berries are pushed down into the syrup with a piece of crumpled parchment paper. Seal containers and freeze. 3 quarts fresh berries will yield about 4 pints frozen.

CHERRIES—Sour cherries do not darken during freezing as sweet cherries do. Simply choose red, ripe, plump cherries and remove all stems. Sort and wash thoroughly. Drain and remove all pits. Pack into containers with 60% syrup. Leave one-inch headspace.

With sweet cherries the procedure is the same except that a 40% syrup is used to which one-half-teaspoon crystalline ascorbic acid (Vitamin C) has been added. This will keep the cherries from changing color and becoming quite unappetizing.

Seal containers, after fruit has been pushed down into syrup, and freeze.

MELONS—In this tasty group are all the favorites including cantaloupe, cranshaw, honeydew, Persian and watermelon, and freezing couldn't be much simpler. Choose ripe melons that have full-colored, firm flesh. Cut in half and remove seeds. Cut the melons into slices or cubes or use a melon baller and make balls.

Discard the rind. Pack into containers and leave headspace. Seal containers and freeze.

PEACHES—These too will change color so a little ascorbic acid is used. Choose fully ripe peaches with no green on the skins. If the peaches are picked off your tree while they are still not quite fully ripe, let them stand and ripen for a day or two.

Sort, wash, pit and peel the peaches. You may slice them or pack them in halves. Put peaches carefully into container with 40% syrup to which one-half-teaspoon crystalline ascorbic acid per quart of syrup has been added. Push fruit down into syrup and leave headspace. Seal containers and freeze.

PEARS—Choose ripe, firm pears. Do not allow to ripen on trees, but pick when mature and ripen indoors. Wash in cold water and peel. Cut in halves or quarters and remove cores. Heat the pears in a 40% syrup for about two minutes, drain off the syrup and cool the pears quickly. Pack the pears cold into containers with cold 40% syrup. Leave headspace. Make certain all fruit is deep in syrup. Seal containers and freeze.

PLUMS—These may be packed in syrup (expecially for desserts) or unsweetened (for jams). For either, choose only deep-colored, ripe, plump fruit. Sort, wash and either leave whole or cut in half and remove pit. In syrup pack, add the fruit to a 50% syrup and seal container after leaving headspace.

To pack unsweetened, simply pack plums into containers leaving one-half-inch headspace; seal and freeze.

RHUBARB—Though not a fruit, rhubarb is packed and frozen as if it were. Choose solid, nicely colored stalks that are young and tender. Wash, trim and cut into pieces. Heat the pieces in boiling water for about one minute. Remove from water and cool immediately. Tightly pack into containers with 40% syrup. Leave headspace. Seal containers and freeze.

STRAWBERRIES—These beauties should be firm and red ripe. Wash berries in cold water, but don't allow them to stand in water. Drain well, sort and remove all hulls. Smaller berries can be left whole. Larger berries are best sliced. Pack berries in containers with cold 50% syrup. Leave headspace. Seal containers and freeze.

If dry sugar pack is preferred, add three-quarters-cup sugar to each quart of strawberries. Turn berries over and over very carefully until most of sugar is dissolved. Take care not to bruise berries as you turn them. Pack berries and juice into containers leaving one-half-inch headspace. Seal containers and freeze.

Whether you decide to freeze or can your produce, or simply cook it your favorite way and eat it as quickly as it becomes ripe, you have much to look forward to in gardening, cooking and preserving. Keep trying. Keep experimenting (within the rules) and . . . best of all . . . ENJOY!!

Index